LINUX FOR BEGINNERS

The Ultimate Crash Course
(2020 Edition)

Mark Solomon Brown

Table of Contents

Introduction

Congratulations on purchasing *Linux for Beginners - The Ultimate Crash Course*! In this book, you can read and find incredibly useful information about one of the most popular operating system worldwide: Linux!

You can learn more about the history of Linux and its retrieval, the most important information about the founder of Linux and a short brief history of operating systems.

You will learn how to install Linux on your computer, and also how to manage hardware and software on your Linux device. You will increase your knowledge because of the most relevant and understandable information and details about how to connect Linux on the internet, using its command line, and how to use Linux distributions properly.

Be assured that after finishing this book, you will be more familiar with using Linux that will lead you to sure success. Enjoy reading!

Mark Solomon Brown

Chapter 1: The history of Linux and Operating Systems

D o you ever imagine how computers or smartphones work and what keeps them "alive"? What engineers need to do to make these devices able to work properly?

The computer's 'life' is known as Operating System...

The first Operating System (OS) was created in 1950s and represents a system software that manages and connects computer hardware and software and produce common services and orders for the computer programs. The operating system can make a task scheduling and keeps the working operations to work flawless during the user's orders.

The operating system is a kind of 'intermediary' between the computer software and hardware and makes every physical instruction in the hardware to be perfectly translated in code that is easy understandable from the computer software, to keep the working on a right way.

There are many operating systems that are used today, but one of them is called Linux.

The family of open-source operating systems - Linux, is built and distributed by Linus Torvalds in 1991. This operating system is packaged with Linux distribution named as Linux Kernel - supporting system software with additional libraries.

Firstly, one operating system named as Unix, was implemented on the marketplace back in 1969. The author of Unix was Dennis Richie and he worked on this operating system in C programming language. Here started the whole story about building better operating system then Unix, called Linux.

In 1990, many of the programs related to computer's software, required an operating system including libraries, compilers, text editors, the famous Unix shell and a windowing system. This all was completed and released with additional low-level elements such as device drivers, daemons and the kernel, called GNU.

A year later in 1991, during his studding to the universe of Helsinki, Linus Torvalds started with Linux development. He worked on his own operating system kernel, which accidentally became the Linux kernel.

Torvalds started the development of the Linux kernel on MINIX and applications programmed in MINIX, were also used on his Linux project. Linus Torvalds's desire was to switch from his original license and developers worked in hope to integrate GNU components with the Linux kernel, making a fully functional and free operating system.

Linux is certainly developed and built for desktop/laptop computers with Intel architecture and after certain period, it was updated for different platforms and other operating systems.

Thanks to that action and his great idea, today Linux operating system is completely free to use and represent the leading open-source operating system and general-purpose operating system too, with billions of users and devices worldwide with market share of 2,18% of the world's usability.

Linus Torvalds

Chapter 2: Linux Comparison With Other Operating Systems

Why to choose Linux operating system beside the others?

S o the answer is very simple and very understandable. There are hundreds of reasons why Linux is more compatible and acceptable for you and your PC working activities. One of the most important is that Linux is an excellent choice for personal Unix computing. If you're a Unix software developer, why use Windows to develop these things? Linux will allow you to develop and test Unix software on your computer, including database and various applications. With Linux, you can run your own Unix system and tailor it to your own needs because it is open-source operating system and you can manage it for your needs and desire.

Many businesses are moving to Linux in other Unix-based workstation environments. Linux has an excellent price performance ratio and this make this operating system one of the most stable and powerful operating systems available and because of its Open Source nature, it is completely customizable for everyone's needs. Universities are finding Linux to be perfect for teaching courses in operating systems design. Larger commercial software companies realized that the opportunities of using a free operating system can be very acceptable and beneficial.

Here are some direct comparisons of Linux with other operating systems...

1. Linux vs Windows 95 and 98

It is not uncommon to run both Linux and Windows 95/98 on the same system. Many Linux users rely on Windows for applications such as word processing and productivity tools. While Linux provides its own analogs for these applications and commercial software support for Linux, there are various reasons why a particular user would want to run Windows as well as Linux.

There are many commercial applications for Windows that aren't available for Linux, and there's no reason why you can't use both.

On the other hand, Linux runs completely in the processor's protected mode and exploits all of the features of the machine, including multiple processors.

However, suffice it to say that Linux and Windows are completely different entities. Compared to other commercial operating systems, Windows is inexpensive and has a strong foothold in the computing world. No other operating system for the PC has reached the level of popularity of Windows, largely because the cost of these other operating systems is very high for most personal computer users. Very few users can imagine spending a thousand dollars or more on the operating system alone. Linux is free, and you can use it and implement it anytime when you need it.

Linux is not for everybody. But if you have always wanted to run a complete Unix system at home, without the high cost, Linux may be what you're looking for.

There are tools available to allow you to interact between Linux and Windows. For example, it's easy to access Windows files from Linux. Development is proceeding on the Wine Windows emulator, which allows you to run many popular applications.

2. Linux vs Windows NT

A number of other advanced operating systems are on the rise in the today's computer world. Microsoft's Windows NT is one of them and becoming very popular for server computing day by day.

Windows NT, like Linux, is a full multitasking operating system with supporting multiprocessor machines and several CPU architectures. It also provides virtual memory, networking, security and so much more. The real difference between Linux and Windows NT is that Linux is a version of Unix and hence benefits from the contributions of the Unix community.

Windows NT, on the other hand, is a proprietary system. The interface and design are controlled by a Microsoft Corporation, and only that corporation may implement the design. In one sense, NT is NT wherever you go.

Linux is also much smaller than Windows NT, has a much better price performance ratio, and is generally seen as more stable. It might seem amazing that for many people's opinion 'small' Linux gives Microsoft serious competition, but it's not surprising when you realize how effective the open-source development process really is.

3. Implementation of Linux/Unix beside other operating systems

First of all, Linux supports a much wider range of hardware than other Unix implementations, simply because there is more demand under Linux to support every crazy brand of sound, graphics, network, and SCSI board. Under the Open Source model, anyone with enough time and interest to write a driver for a particular board is able to do it.

The most important reason to consider many of the users is price. The Linux software is free if you have access to the

Internet and you can easily download it on your device. If you do not have access to such a network, you may need to purchase it via mail or order on CD-ROM, and such packages often include bundled documentation and support.

Of course, you may copy Linux from a friend who may already have the software or share the cost of purchasing it with someone else. If you are planning to install Linux on a large number of machines, you need only purchase a single copy of the software and you can do the rest of the work properly and legally.

There are other free or inexpensive implementations of Unix nowadays. One of the most well-known implement is FreeBSD, an implementation and port of BSD Unix. FreeBSD is comparable to Linux in many ways but deciding which one is "better" depends on your own needs and expectations.

Other inexpensive versions of Unix is Minix. Some of these implementations are the mostly for academic interest, while others are full-fledged systems for real productivity.

4. Why Linux is more secure than other operating system

Linux is an open-source operating system and the codes which can be read by everyone. This operating system still accept more secure in comparison with other Operating Systems. Linux is growing rapidly in the market because there are more devices based on Linux, and that is why more people trust Linux.

In Windows operating system, users by default have access to everything in the system because they are given administrator rights. If the virus will be able to pass their system, they can quickly gain access to important parts of the system. On the other hand, in Linux, they have a lower access rights, and the virus can only access local files and folders, the system will remain safe.

Windows and other operating systems are more vulnerabilities to the type of social engineering Ltd compared to Linux. Incompetent users can easily download a virus by simply opening an attachment in e-mail. Of course, this is not the case of Linux, when users are more technically savvy, and are unlikely to access and download such suspicious attachments. They also need to give the rights to execution, so unlikely to happen real damage. Various developers and testers working on Linux, so, as soon as there is some kind of vulnerability, it will be quickly found and fixed, unlike other operating systems.

An even higher level of security on Linux machines is implemented using IPtables. This is a protection that allows you to create a more secure environment for the execution of any command or access the network. Linux works in many environments such as Linux Mint, Debian, Ubuntu, Gentoo, Arch, and many others. Various email clients, environment console and system packages also make the system difficult for any virus attack. The architecture of Windows is not so divided, so a virus could easily reach the many computers of the system which will cause harm to their users.

Linux accesses to files and system accesses are written to a log file. If someone tries to enter safe system files, these system gaps can be viewed by the system administrator. Written to the disk failed login attempts and other security issues, all of this is available for reviewing later.

Chapter 3: Linux installing

As we already know, Linux is free open-source operating system and you can download and install it on your device anytime. There are so many Linux distributions out there, so you can choose one and install it on your computer, for example Ubuntu, Fedora, Linux Mint, Gentoo and more...

If you decide to install Linux operating system on your PC, you can do it on 3 ways. The first way is via USB installer, the second one is via CD ROM and the third one is with Virtual installation.

1. Linux installation with USB

The best version or distribution from Linux operating system is Ubuntu looking the data of the market share, so here is the following steps how to install it on your device.

Step 1. You need to download the Linux operating system file on your computer. The file extension is .iso or something similar depending of the version and distribution type. You can easily find Ubuntu or other distribution for desktop purpose.

Step 2. After downloading the Operating System file .iso, you can also download the UUI (Universal USB Installer) which is free software to make a compatible USB stick access. The downloading window for UUI looks like the following picture:

Step 3. Next, you should select your relevant Linux distribution from the first gap in the working window. When you choose your one, you need to decide where your

distribution to be installed on your device, and to put everything in action, you should press the 'create' button below. This action is represented on the picture below:

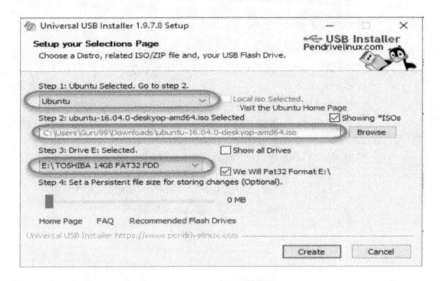

Step 4. After clicking on the 'create' button, you need to click 'YES' button from the following opened window. This window is from Universal USB Installer - Setup. Here is the example of that Setup window:

Universal USB Installer 1.9.7.8 Setup

WARNING: Backup any data on this drive before proceeding! All existing data (including any other volumes, partitions, and associated drive letters on this drive), will be destroyed.

Universal USB Installer is Ready to perform the following actions:

1.) Lock and Dismount Disk - Allows (E:) to be wiped, cleaned, and partitioned.

2.) Fat32 Format (E:) - All Data (including any other volumes, partitions, and associated drive letters on this drive) will be Irrecoverably Deleted!

3.) Create a Syslinux MBR on (E:) - Existing MBR will be Overwritten!

4.) Create UUI Label on (E:) - Existing Label will be Overwritten!

5.) Install ubuntu-16.04.0-deskyop-amd64 on (E:)

Are you absolutely positive this Drive is your USB Device?
Double Check with Windows (My Computer) to make sure!

Click YES to perform these actions on (E:) or NO to Abort!

Yes   No

Step 5. Congrats! Your chosen Linux distribution will be ready to go very soon. After the finishing of installation process, you will be able to use this operative system on your computer.

2. Linux installation with CD-ROM

If you are a CD lover or want to take computer action with classic CD method, then you should use the second method for Linux operating system installing and that is installing with using Linux CD ROM. Here are the steps how to do it easily and less frustrating.

Step 1. Both first steps in Linux installing with USB or with CD ROM are the same. First you need to download the Linux Operating System file or your computer with file extension .iso or similar depending on the distribution type. Ubuntu is the best version and the most used by the Linux users.

Step 2. After downloading the Linux operating system file, you need to put the CD ROM on your device, of course. There will be an icon or shortcut on the desktop and you need to activate it. Here is an example of the CD shortcut:

Step 3. Follow and fill the continuing gaps and your operating system will be installed for a certain period of time.

3. Linux installation using Virtual Machine

Virtual machine Linux installing is a very popular method to install a Linux operating system. The virtual installation offers you the freedom of running Linux on an existing Operating System already installed on your computer. This means if you have Windows operating system on your computer, then you can just run Linux with a click of a button. Let's see the steps how to do it in details.

Step 1. Download and install Virtual Box. Depending on your processor and Operating System, select the appropriate package. Here is the picture as an example:

Step 2. Open the downloaded file, double click on Setup file and click 'Next'.

Step 3. Select your location directory where to install Virtual Box and click on 'Next'.

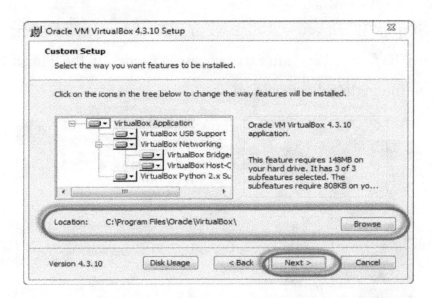

Step 4. After that, click on 'Install' on the continuing window.

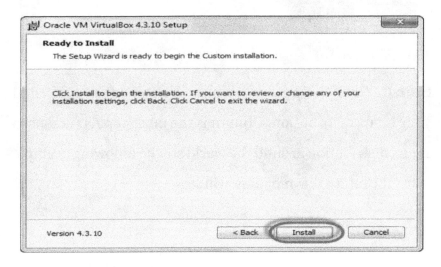

Step 5. When you will click on the 'Instal' button, installing will be finished and after that you need to click on the 'Finish' button in the following window.

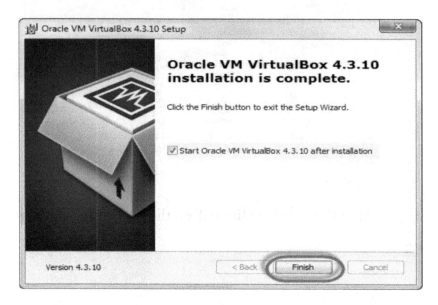

Step 6. When this process is finished, now you need to install your Linux distribution. Ubuntu is the most popular and used Linux distribution around the world so, the following example is from Ubuntu downloading window.

Step 7. Now, you need to create a machine in your Virtual Box. Open up the Virtual Box and click on the button 'New' in the top left corner.

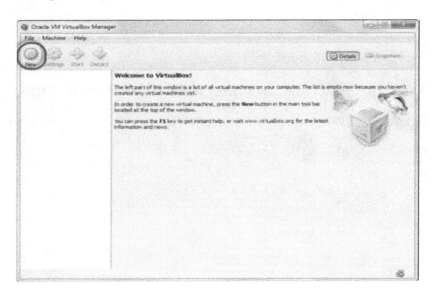

Step 8. In the next window, type a name of your Operating System which you are installing in Virtual Box, select Linux and distribution with 32 bit. Click on 'Next'

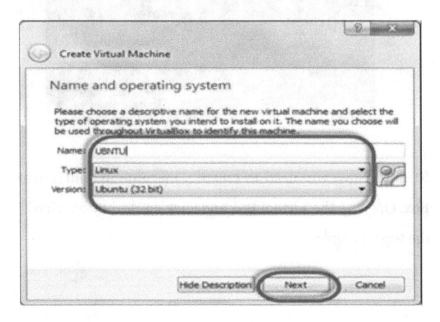

Step 9. After that, allocate RAM size to your Virtual Operating System. I recommend keeping 1024mb (1 GB) and click on 'Next'.

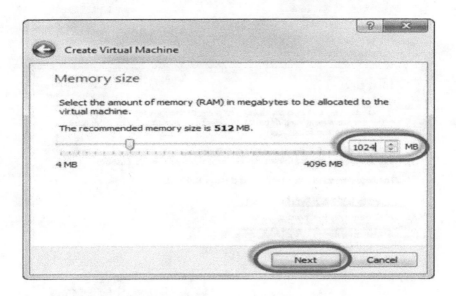

Step 10. Now, you need to run the Operating System in Virtual Box. You have to create virtual hard disk. Click on 'Create a virtual hard drive now' and click on 'Create'. The virtual hard disk is where the Operating System installation files and data you create or install in this machine depending on your Linux distribution choice.

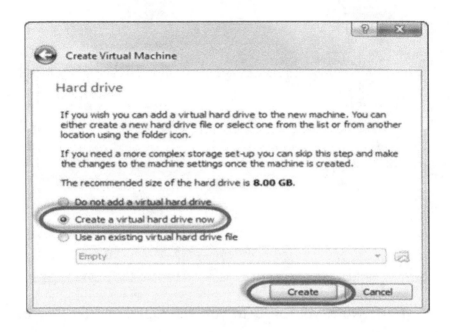

Step 11. After that, select VHD (Virtual Hard Disk) option. You can choose the type of file that you would like to use on the new created Virtual Hard Disk. When you pick and fill the certain field, click on 'Next' button.

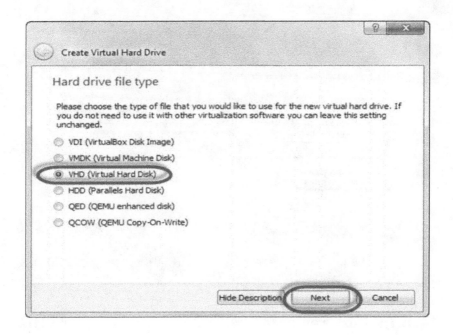

Step 12. When the next window comes up, click on 'dynamic allocated' and click on 'Next'. This means that the size of the disk will increase dynamically, per requirement.

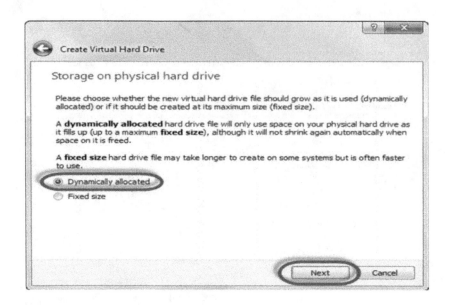

Step 13. Next, you need to allocate memory on your VHD. 8GB recommended.

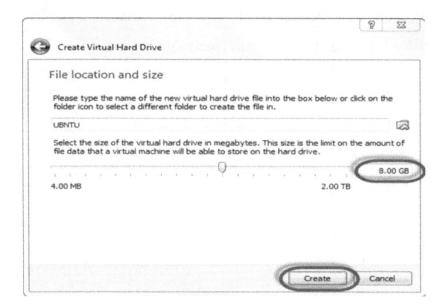

Step 14. Now, you have to install your chosen Linux distribution on your virtual machine. Select the machine and click on green 'Start'. Here is the example of Ubuntu installation.

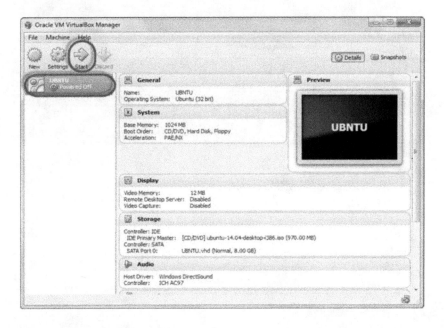

Step 15. After that, you need to select the folder option and pick the place where you want the Linux distribution to be installed in your device disk. Just pick the location and click on 'Start' button.

Step 16. On the next window, click on the Linux distribution .iso file and after that, click 'Open' button.

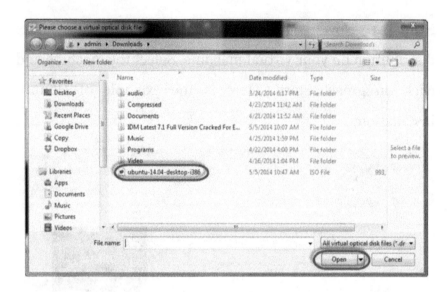

Step 17. After that, you will have 2 options to run your distribution and you need to click on 'Install Ubuntu'. Ubuntu is distribution example here, but you can choose your one.

Step 18. On the next opened window, click 'Continue' button.

Step 19. After clicking on 'Continue' button, on the next window, you need to select option to erase the disk and install your chosen Linux distribution with one click on 'Install Now' button. This option installs Ubuntu or your chosen distribution into your virtual hard drive which is created earlier.

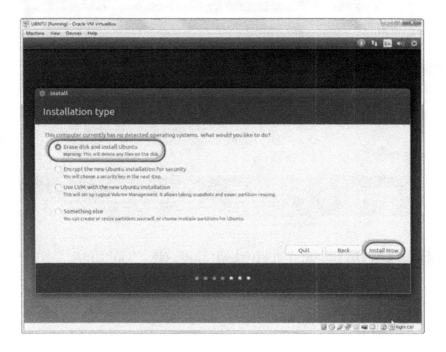

Step 20. After that action and at the end of this process, you can set up the time zone, pick a language and create your user name, password and other login information. With clicking on the 'Continue' button, the installation process will start and for a short period of time it will be fully done.

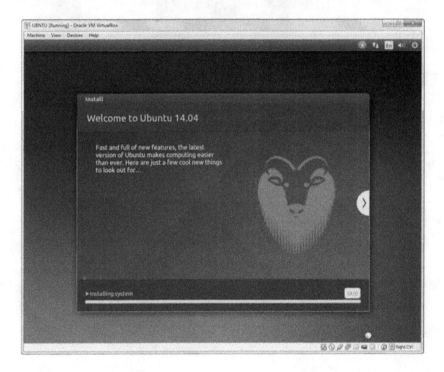

Chapter 4: How To Get Started With Linux

You are finished with downloading and installing method for your chosen Linux distribution or Linux operating system. After the whole process of adjusting your computer for the new operating system, you need to set up the Linux performances and environment related to your needs and working opportunities.

Depending on which Linux distribution and desktop environment you choose, your desktop environment and installed applications will vary. Most of them will cover your typical needs and similar personal requirement based on computer working. Most Linux distributions are connected with the Firefox web browser and the open-source Chromium browser or Google Chrome is just a few clicks away.

Your desktop environment should have all the standards. The application menu, some sort of taskbar and a notification area or "system tray." You should also find a collection of system services that will help you to configure your hardware and make your desktop work properly on the right way.

Ubuntu 16.04's Unity desktop can be quirky, but it's packed with useful features you'd never find on your own, like the HUD. If you're going with Ubuntu 16.04 or earlier, be aware that Ubuntu will be abandoning its Unity desktop in future versions. Ubuntu dropped Unity in favor of the GNOME shell that comes default on Fedora and other distributions. If you want to try Ubuntu, we recommend trying Ubuntu GNOME, which uses the GNOME desktop instead of Unity.

If you're unhappy with the desktop you're using, don't worry. While some distributions are optimized for a particular desktop, nearly every major distribution gives you the option to install the desktop of your choice after the system is installed. As long as you have enough storage to spare, you can have GNOME, KDE, Cinnamon, XFCE, and other desktops installed at the same time. When you log in to the desktop, you can choose what desktop environment to run.

Generally, you can find a lot of information on Google for your distribution's name followed by the question that will lead you in the right direction. If you prefer a more structured help environment, the Ubuntu and Fedora documentation websites are great resources. While the Arch Wiki is written with users of Arch Linux in mind, it is a great in-depth resource for Linux programs in general.

You have choices about when and how to install Linux. You can leave it on a disc or USB drive and boot it up whenever you want to play with it. Play with it several times until you're sure you want to install it. You can try several Linux distributions in this way and you can even reuse the same USB drive.

The big reasons to install Linux instead of just running it from a USB drive or virtual disc are productivity and convenience. Installed Linux will remember your settings, keep your installed software, and maintain your files between reboots.

Once you feel ready to take the plunge, installing Linux on your PC is easy. Just launch the installer provided in the Linux environment. You could wipe away your existing Windows system and replace it with Linux, but installing it in a "dual-boot" configuration, or in Ubuntu installer parlance. The installer will resize your Windows partition to make room for Linux and you can select which operating system you want to use every time you boot your computer. Of course, you can always choose to install Windows in a virtual machine as well.

Software installation on Linux works very differently from software installation on Windows. You don't need to open your web browser and search for applications. Instead, look for the software installer on your system. On Ubuntu and Fedora, you can install software using GNOME's software store application.

Your Linux distribution hosts its own "software repositories," containing software compiled to work with it. This software is tested and provided by the Linux distribution. If security patches are necessary, your Linux distribution will provide them to you in a standard way.

While most major distributions offer GUI programs to help you install software, all distributions have command-line tools that can do the same thing. Though it can be intimidating for newbies, we recommend users familiarize themselves with how to install applications from the command line, even if they prefer using the GUI. If an installation fails for some reason, using the command line will offer hints as to why the installation failed.

To recap, a distribution is a Linux operating system that ships with all the software needed to provide you with a complete experience. They provide the kernel along with hardware drivers and applications.

Distributions come in all shapes and sizes. Some are aimed at newcomers, while others are geared toward the most diehard of command line junkies. Ubuntu, Fedora, and openSUSE are three general purpose distributions good for people of all skill levels.

There are many other Linux distributions available, and each one is a bit different. Some distributions are fine set to serve a particular niche. This way you can install an operating system that was built for multimedia creation or one that was created for computers with old or underpowered hardware.

On that note, hardware compatibility is perhaps the most important thing to consider when switching to Linux. While most hardware is supported by default in the majority of

Linux distributions, less popular or quirky hardware might not work. Most of the times, even if your device isn't supported by default, you can follow online tutorials that take you through installing an unsupported driver or patching the kernel — but that's not a task suited for everyone.

Some applications particularly closed applications like Google Chrome, Steam, Skype, Minecraft, and others may have to be installed from outside your Linux distribution's package manager. Check your package manager first and see what apps may be available through your repositories.

If you can't find the app you need, you can download these applications from their official websites, just as you would on Windows. Be sure to download the installer package designed for the Linux distribution you are using.

Open source software doesn't cost money, and everyone is free to look at the source code and modify it as they please. This means that skilled developers from around the world contribute their work either for free or via sponsorship from companies like Canonical or Red Hat. But you can improve the software as well.

In contrast, the Windows source code is not available to anyone but Microsoft employees. You can't build your own Windows kernel, fix bugs, or distribute an improved version of Windows that you created.

Linux is different, and the GNU General Public License is part of the reason why this license provides the legal grounds for your rights to the software. It ensures that even when a work is modified or enhanced, it still remains in the public domain for other people to use and enjoy. It is the most widely used license in the common community.

It is hard to imagine how many people use Linux today. The rank on the popularity of each distribution's website is really wide and large. This gives an impression of what people are interested in, but it is hardly to represent of which distributions are the most used worldwide. Ubuntu, for example, is not currently ranked as number one, but it is widely considered the most popular version of desktop Linux.

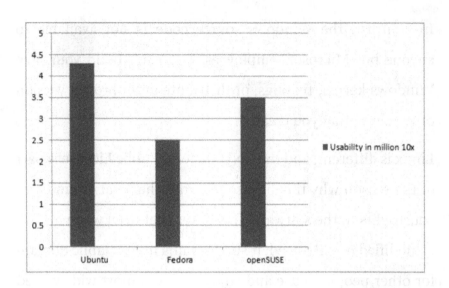

Chapter 5: Linux Architecture and Distributions

The free software movement began in 1983 when Richard Stallman launched the GNU Project. GNU, is a recursive acronym that stands for GNU is not Unix. His goal was to create a totally free and open source GNU operating system compatible with Unix. He and other software developers started on this project by recreating the most popular Unix commands. By 1990 all the major components of the operating system had been written with one big exception, the kernel.

One of the things that set Linux apart from other operating systems is the way software is installed and managed. Traditionally, when you wanted to install software on the Windows operating system you would find the software, download the software, and install the software. These are steps that the end user has to perform one-by-one. Imaging browsing the web for an application, downloading that application to your "Downloads" folder, double clicking on the download setup shortcut to start the installation process and then answering a series of questions to finally install the software.

To install software on a Linux system you can use the package manager that comes with the distribution. To install a new piece of software you search for it and install it from the operating system itself. The package manager takes care of downloading the software along and then install all of the components. They can also manage the operating system itself. A package manager can update and upgrade the system and all of its installed applications to latest versions.

Software and applications are handled into packages and Linux distributions are categorized by these package types. The three basic types of packages are Debian (deb), Red Hat Package Manager (RPM), and other distributions.

1. Debian package distributions

The Debian package type was created in 1993 for the Debian Linux distribution. Debian is one of the oldest Linux distributions and it is very popular choice on which new distributions are based. Popular distributions that use .deb packages are:

- Debian

- Ubuntu

- Linux Mint

- Steam OS

Debian

Debian is developed in 1993 by Ian Murdock who announced a new Linux distribution that was developed openly with the GNU philosophy. Ian gave his distribution the name Debian which is a combination of his girlfriend's name Debra and his own name. At first it was a small project, but today Debian is one of biggest open source projects in today's marketplace.

Debian is an universal operating system and supports almost all CPU architectures and it is a very popular in the server space. Although this distribution is known for rock solid stable software, there are various types. There is Debian old stable, stable, testing, unstable and experimental. As you go from old stable to experimental, you will find newer and less stable software. As for package management, Debian uses two package managers, apt and aptitude.

This distribution has access to online repositories that contain over 51,000 packages. Debian officially contains only free software, but non-free software can be downloaded and installed from the Debian repositories, including popular free programs such as LibreOffice, Firefox web browser, Evolution mail, VLC media player, GIMP image editor, Evince document viewer and so on. Debian is a popular choice for servers, for example as the operating system component of a LAMP stack.

Several parts of Debian are translated into languages other than American English, including package descriptions, configuration messages, documentation and the website.

The level of software localization depends on the language, ranging from the highly supported German and French to the barely translated. The Debian 10 installer is available in 76 languages.

Ubuntu

Created in 2004, Ubuntu is based on Debian unstable. Ubuntu is the most widely used and most popular Linux distribution today. Ubuntu started with the GNOME desktop, but a few years ago Ubuntu developed its own desktop environment named Unity. The Ubuntu installation process is easy and popular with those new methods to Linux. This distribution uses apt and its graphical fronted Ubuntu Software Center for package management.

Ubuntu is named after the African philosophy, which Canonical translates as "humanity to others" or "I am what I am because of who we all are". Ubuntu is built on Debian's architecture and infrastructure, and comprises Linux server, desktop and discontinued phone and tablet operating system versions. Ubuntu releases updated versions predictably every six months and each release receives free support for nine months with security fixes, high impact bug fixes and conservative, substantially beneficial low-risk bug fixes.

A default installation of Ubuntu contains a wide range of software that includes Libre Office, Firefox, Thunderbird, Transmission, and several lightweight games such as Sudoku and chess. Many additional software packages are accessible from the built in Ubuntu Software as well as any other package management tools. Many additional software packages that are no longer installed by default, such as Evolution, GIMP, Pidgin, and Synaptic are still accessible and still installable by the main tool or by any other APT-based package management tool.

Ubuntu mentality is to be secure by default. User's programs run with low privileges and can't corrupt the operating system or other users' files. For increased security, tool is used to assign temporary privileges for performing administrative tasks, which allows the root account to remain locked and helps prevent inexperienced users from unintentionally making the system changes or opening security holes. Polkit is also being widely implemented into the desktop.

Most network ports are closed by default to prevent hacking. A built-in firewall allows the users who install network servers to control access. Ubuntu compiles its packages using GCC features such as PIE and buffer overflow protection to harden its software.

Ubuntu also supports full disk encryption as well as encryption of the home and Private directories. As Ubuntu is distributed freely and there is no registration process, this distribution usage can only be roughly estimated. In 2015, looking the data from market share analytics, Ubuntu now has over 40 million desktop users and counting.

Linux Mint

Linux Mint is a popular distribution based on Ubuntu. Linux Mint started out simply being Ubuntu with pre-installed multimedia codecs and proprietary drivers. However, it has since grown and is a very popular alternative to Ubuntu. Linux Mint provides full out-of-the-box multimedia support by including some proprietary software and comes bundled with a variety of free and open-source applications.

Linux Mint primarily uses free and open-source software, making exceptions for some proprietary software, such as plug-ins and codecs that provide Adobe Flash, MP3, and DVD playback. Linux Mint's inclusion of proprietary software is unusual. Many Linux distributions do not include proprietary software by default, as a common goal for some Linux distributions is to connect to the model of free and open-source software.

Linux Mint comes with a wide range of software installed that includes Libre Office, Firefox, Thunderbird, Hex Chat, Pidgin, Transmission, VLC media player and GIMP. Additional software that is not installed by default can be downloaded using the package manager.

In 2010, Linux Mint released Linux Mint Debian Edition (LMDE). Unlike the other Ubuntu-based editions, Linux Mint Debian Edition was originally a rolling release based directly on Debian and was not tied to Ubuntu packages or its release schedule.

Every version of Linux Mint is given a version number and it was code-named with a feminine first name ending in "a" and beginning with a letter of the alphabet that increased with every iteration. The 18.x series broke from the pattern with version 18 having the name "Sarah".

Initially, there were two Linux Mint releases per year. Following the release of Linux Mint 5 in 2008, every fourth release was labeled a long-term support (LTS) version, indicating that it was supported with updates for longer than traditional releases. Versions 5 and 9 had three years of support, and all long term support versions following received five years of support.

The most poopular Linux Mint software is Cinnamon. Cinnamon is a fork of GNOME Shell based on the innovations made in Mint Gnome Shell Extensions (MGSE). It has been released as an additionally part for Linux Mint 12 and available as a default desktop environment since Linux Mint 13.

Linux Mint does not communicate specific release dates as new versions are published when were fully ready, meaning that they can be released early when the distribution is ahead of schedule or late when critical bugs are found. New releases are announced, with much other material on the Linux Mint website and blog.

Linux Mint software tools are: Software Manager (mint Install), Update Manager (mint Update), Main Menu (mint Menu), Backup Tool (mint Backup), Upload Manager (mint Upload), Domain Blocker (mint Nanny), Desktop Settings (mint Desktop), Welcome Screen (mint Welcome), USB

Image Writer/USB Stick Formatter (mint Stick), System Reports (mint Report).

Steam OS

SteamOS is the primary operating system for the Steam Machine gaming platform by Valve Corporation. It is based on Debian Linux. It was released alongside the start of user beta testing of Steam Machines in December 2013.

During a panel at LinuxCon in 2013, Valve co-founder and executive director Gabe Newell stated that he believed Linux and open source are the future of gaming. His opinion was that the company is aiding game developers who want to make games compatible with Linux and they would be making an announcement related to introducing Linux in front of the people.

In October 2013, Valve announced Steam Developers Days and two-day developer conference where video game developers will be able to test and provide feedback on SteamOS and Steam Machines. In October 2013, Nvidia also announced their collaboration with Valve to support SteamOS with the help of a development suite called Nvidia Game

Works which incorporates PhysX, OptiX, VisualFX and other Nvidia proprietary APIs and implementations.

On the official release of Steam Machines in November 2015, Ars Technica compared the rendering performance of cross-platform games on Steam OS and Windows 10 running on the same machine, using average frame per second measurements, and found that the games were rendered between 21% and 58% slower on SteamOS compared to Windows 10. Ars Technica considered this might be due to the inexperience of developers optimizing on OpenGL in contrast to DirectX, and believed that the performance might improve with future titles. Ars Technica noted that its benchmark, comprising only six games on a single computer, was far from comprehensive.

The SteamOS beta release received mixed reviews. In Tech Radar's review they see how easy is to navigate interface and future potential but criticized the hard installation and lack of extra features compared to the Steam software.

Thomas Morgan, from Eurogamer, did not incur installation problems however commented negatively on the lack of options available for detecting monitor resolutions and audio output and the lack of games available natively on the operating system. He did, however, also respond positively to the user interface and called it "a positive start".

Since then, outlets such as Ars Technica have revisited the SteamOS since its initial debut, offering observations on the platform's growth, pros, and cons. Both Falcon Northwest and Origin PC, computer manufacturers that were planning on offering Steam Machine hardware, opted to not ship a SteamOS enabled machine in 2015 due to limitations of SteamOS over Windows. Falcon Northwest had said that they will still consider shipping machines with SteamOS in the future if performance improves.

2. Red Hat package distributions

RedHat package manager is a free and open source package management system. The name RPM refers to .rpm file format and the package manager program itself. RPM was intended primarily for Linux distributions and the file format is the baseline package format of the Linux Standard Base. RedHat created the package format for use in its distribution. Popular RPM based distributions are:

- RedHat Enterprise Linux (RHEL)

- CentOS

- Fedora

- OpenSuse

- Mageia

RedHat Enterprise Linux (RHEL)

Red Hat Enterprise Linux is the world's leading enterprise Linux platform. It is an open source operating system (OS). It is the foundation from which you can scale existing apps and roll out emerging technologies across bare-metal, virtual, container, and all types of cloud environments.

For a system administrator performing software installation and maintenance, the use of package management rather than manual building has advantages such as simplicity, consistency and the ability for these processes to be automated and non-interactive.

Features of RPM are including RPM packages (cryptographically verified with GPG and MD5), original source archive, automatic build-time dependency evaluation and so on.

Administrators can set up algorithmic criteria using system-wide security policies so, apps automatically use the appropriate cryptographic package. And each subscription comes with Red Hat Insights, a predictive IT analytics service that identifies potential issues before they become problems.

Built in management components include a user-friendly web console and application streams, let you offer multiple app versions to multiple users. Connect Red Hat Enterprise Linux with Red Hat Smart Management to control your standard operating environments on site and across clouds.

In a UNIX environment, providing access based on locally stored information becomes unmanageable as the number of systems and users increases. Storing the user information in a Lightweight Directory Access Protocol (LDAP) based directory, Red Hat Directory Server makes the system scalable, manageable, and secure.

Red Hat gives you centralized, fine-grained access control, including control based on user identity, group membership, role identity, IP address, domain name, or pattern-based rules. Restrict access to directory data with control down to the attribute value level.

Cent OS

CentOS or Community Enterprise Operating System is a Linux distribution that provides a free, community-supported computing platform compatible with its upstream source Red Hat Enterprise Linux (RHEL). In January 2014, CentOS announced the official joining with Red Hat while staying independent under a new CentOS governing board. The first CentOS was released in May 2004, numbered as CentOS version 2.

In July 2010, CentOS overtook Debian to become the most popular Linux distribution for web servers, with almost 30% of all Linux web servers using it. Soon after that, Debian retook the lead in January 2012.

CentOS developers use Red Hat's source code to create a final product very similar to Red Hat Enterprise Linux. Red Hat's branding and logos are changed because Red Hat does not allow them to be redistributed and set up seriously copyrights. CentOS is available free of charge. Technical support is primarily provided by the community via official mailing lists, web forums and chatting platforms.

Fedora

Fedora is a Linux distribution developed by the community-supported Fedora Project and sponsored primarily by Red Hat. Fedora contains software distributed under various free and open-source licenses and aims to be on the leading edge of today's popular technologies. Fedora is the upstream source of the commercial Red Hat Enterprise Linux distribution.

Since the release of Fedora 21, different editions are currently available on the marketplace, such as: Workstation focused on the personal computer, Server for servers, and Atomic focused on cloud computing.

As of February 2016, Fedora has an estimated 1.2 million users, including Linus Torvalds, creator of the Linux kernel.

Fedora has a reputation for focusing on innovation, integrating new technologies early on and working closely with upstream Linux communities. Making changes upstream instead of specifically for Fedora ensures that the changes are available to all Linux distributions.

Fedora has a relatively short life cycle: each version is usually supported for at least 13 months, where version X is supported only until 1 month after version X+2 is released. Fedora users can upgrade from version to version without reinstalling.

Fedora uses Security-Enhanced Linux by default, which implements a variety of security policies, including mandatory access controls, which Fedora adopted early on. Fedora provides hardening wrapper, and does hardening for all of its packages by using compiler features such as position-independent executable.

This distribution comes preinstalled with a wide range of software such as Libre Office and Firefox. Additional software is available from the software repositories and can be installed using the DNF package manager or GNOME Software. GNOME Software is Fedora's default package manager.

Additionally, extra repositories can be added to the system, so that software not available in Fedora can be installed easily. Fedora also provides users with an easy to use build system for creating their own repositories. Since the release of Fedora 25, the operating system defaults to the Wayland display server protocol, which replaced the X Window System.

Fedora is the upstream of the commercial RedHat Enterprise Linux distribution, or RHEL for short. What makes Fedora special is it uses newer technology and packages from the open source world than RHEL. Fedora, like Red Hat Enterprise Linux, uses the package manager.

The default desktop environment in Fedora is GNOME and the default user interface is the GNOME Shell. Other desktop environments, including KDE Plasma, Xfce, LXDE, MATE, Deepin and Cinnamon, are available and can be installed by your desire.

OpenSUSE

OpenSUSE or SUSE Linux is a Linux distribution sponsored by SUSE Linux and other companies. It is widely used throughout the world. The focus of its development is creating usable open-source tools for software developers and system administrators, while providing a user-friendly desktop and feature rich server environment.

Novell created openSUSE after purchasing SuSE Linux for $210 million dollars on 4th of November 2003. The Attachmate Group acquired Novell and SUSE into two autonomous subsidiary companies. After The Attachmate Group merged with Micro Focus in November 2014, SUSE became its own business unit. On 4th July 2018, EQT Partners purchased SUSE for $2.5 billion dollars.

Beyond the distributions and tools, the openSUSE provides a web portal for community involvement. The community develops openSUSE collaboration with its corporate sponsors through the Open Build Service, writing documentation, designing artwork, fostering discussions on open mailing lists and in Internet Relay Chat channels.

Like most Linux distributions, openSUSE includes both a default graphical user interface (GUI) and a command line interface option. Users of openSUSE may choose several desktops environments like: GNOME, KDE, Cinnamon, MATE, LXQt, Xfce and others.

OpenSUSE is fully and freely available for immediate download and is also sold in retail box to the general public. It comes in several editions for the various architectures, like:

- openSUSE Leap

- openSUSE Tumbleweed

- openSUSE Factory

- openSUSE Retail Edition

OpenSuse started out a German translation of Slackware Linux, but eventually grew into its own distribution. OpenSuse is known for the KDE desktop and stability too.

Mageia

Mageia is a Linux-based operating system, distributed as free and open source software. It was forked from the Mandriva Linux distribution. The term Mageia means enchantment, fascination, glamour, style and similar. The first release of the software distribution, Mageia 1 was in June 2011.

Mageia was created in 2010 as a distribution of Mandriva Linux, by a group of former employees of Mandriva and several other developers and users of the Mandriva community.

On 2nd of September 2010, Edge IT one of the subsidiaries of Mandriva, was placed under liquidation process on 17th of September and all assets were liquidated and employees were released.

The next day, on 18th of September 2010, some of these former employees, who were mostly responsible for the development and maintenance of the Mandriva Linux distribution and several community members announced the creation of Mageia, with the support of many members of the community users and employees of Mandriva Linux.

Mageia can use all major desktop environments. As was the case with Mandrake and Mandriva Linux, KDE is the main and the most used environment. Users can choose from KDE and GNOME 64 bit DVD editions and much more. It uses Mageia Control Center. The Linux softwares like LXDE, LXQt, Cinnamon, MATE and similar are also available.

Mageia was planned originally to be released on a 9-month release cycle, with each release to be supported for 18 months.

Actual practice has been to release a new version when the Mageia development community feels the new release is ready from quality and stability viewpoints.

The latest stable version is Mageia 7.1, released in July 2019.

3. Other Linux popular distributions

There are several Linux operating system distributions that are widely used around the world and have a lot of supporters because of their creation, development and design.

Here are some of them...

Arch Linux

Arch Linux has its own package manager called pacman. Arch does not come with a graphical installer and the whole installation process is done via a terminal. This can be intimidating for new Linux users. The main philosophy behind Arch is KISS or Keep It Simple Stupid. Arch has been forked in some popular beginner friendly distributions such as Manjaro Linux and similar.

Slackware

Founded in 1992 by Patrick Volkerding, Slackware is the oldest Linux distribution in use today. Slackware does not have a package manager and all the software is compiled by the system administrator or normal users of the system. Slackware packages are simply source code. If you really want to know the first basics of Linux working, use Slackware.

Gentoo

Gentoo is based on the portage package management system. This distribution can be difficult to install and can even take a couple of days to complete the entire installation process. The advantage of such an approach is that the software is built for the specific hardware that it will be running on. Like Slackware, Portage uses application source code. If you like the idea of Gentoo, but are looking for something beginner friendly, try Sabayon and start with introducing in the Linux operating system world.

KDE

KDE was created in 1996 and is probably the most advanced desktop manager on the market. By default KDE includes several applications that every user needs for a complete desktop environment. This distribution has some features that are not available in other desktop managers. The KDE workspace is called Plasma. Combining Plasma with the other KDE applications will give you what KDE software compilation.

The most popular distributions that use KDE are:

- OpenSuse

- Slackware

- Linux Mint

- Kubuntu

- Mageia

GNOME

GNOME is an desktop manager made for the Linux community and by the Linux community. This is a great example of how the open source community works. This distribution can easily be expanded with the use of plug-ins.

It does not require a lot of resources and can be a great choice for older and slower hardware.

The most popular distributions that use GNOME are:

- Debian

- OpenSuse

- Fedora

- CentOS

Cinnamon

Cinnamon is a free and open-source desktop environment for the X Window System that derives from GNOME 3 but follows traditional desktop metaphor conventions. Cinnamon is the principal desktop environment of the Linux Mint distribution and is available as an optional desktop for other Linux distributions and other Unix-like operating systems as well. It recreates the look of GNOME 2 with an modern touch. The minimum system requirements for Cinnamon are the same as they are for GNOME.

Xfce

Xfce is an excellent choice for older computers. Light and fast are Xfce's two biggest features. The system requirements are a measly 300Mhz CPU and 192Mb of RAM.

The most popular Linux distributions that use Xfce are:

- Debian

- Xubuntu

- Fedora

- OpenSuse

LXDE

LXDE is another fast and light desktop manager. Based on the Open Box windows manager, LXDE is suitable for old computers.

The most popular Linux distributions that use LXDE are:

- Lubuntu

- Debian

- OpenSuse

- Linux Mint

Unity

Unity was developed by Canonical for their Ubuntu Linux distribution. Till today, Ubuntu is the only distribution that uses Unity. Unity requires greater hardware resources than most graphical environments. You will need 1 GHz CPU and 1Gb RAM in order to get Unity to work. With those specs, Unity will be so slow that it's almost unusable. For Unity, the more RAM and CPU you owned, the better will be the performances and productivity.

To make a summary, there are so many distributions that you can install and download on your computer. You can choose your distribution from the huge pallet of Linux distributions that are represent of the tech marketplace. You can choose between Debian based and Red Hat based Linux distributions, depending on your expectations, needs, working opportunities and personal desires.

Chapter 6: How to choose Linux distribution

Choosing a Linux distribution can be one of the most difficult things for one Linux user. There are so many excellent options, and they all have their own unique and strong performances. There are also constant updates, news and general community data that set up barriers or even more, making the process much less of a direct route. All you can do is to see the right opportunity on the Linux market share and make a good choice related to your needs and expectations. Every distribution is good. Sure, running Arch on your enterprise scale production deployment probably is not the best idea, but it is still technically possible. The point here is all about picking a distribution that fits around that sweet spot of what you want and need.

Do you want to run a certain distribution on a desktop PC or server? The needs of these situations are very different. Server distributions need to be solid stable, while it is probably better to have updated software on a desktop.

If you are planning on running a server, you are looking for a long release cycles, compatible versions of the software you plan on deploying and support.

For desktops, you don't need long release cycles. You probably want newer versions of your applications. You might even want a release that always keeps you on the edge. Sure, you also want some stability, but it is not so critical. You will also like a graphical desktop environment. Distribution that provides something that you find visually pleasing is all you need, and you certainly don't want something different and weird.

If you want to run Linux on your desktop computer then you need to ask yourself another technology question. Do you want something simple or something more advanced? Many Linux distributions, like Ubuntu, aim to be as user friendly as much as possible and easy to manage too. They don't serve you with a lot of choice, but they just work when you install them.

In contrast, there are distributions like Gentoo and Arch Linux that everything is about your personal choice. They let you do whatever you want with your system, including breaking it in a new and creative ways. These distributions put all the control in your hands and you can create some spectacular custom-tailored results, but they also leave a lot of failure and they take time to maintain and fix.

Don't let the beginner designation make your activities difficult. A lot of Linux experts opt for distributions like Ubuntu because they work and are professional. If you have got a work to do most of the time, it is the best to pick something that lets you get that job done with as little headache as possible.

Beginner friendly Linux distributions:

- Ubuntu

- Linux Mint

- Fedora

- SolusOS

- ElementaryOS

- OpenSUSE

Advanced Linux distributions:

- Debian,

- OpenSUSE

- Tumbleweed

- Arch Linux

- Gentoo

- Slackware

Once you have decided what type of Linux distribution you want to use on your computer, beginner or advanced distribution, there are a couple of major factors to consider that set them apart.

The first thing that you need to consider in picking a distribution is which software is available in its repositories. If a distribution doesn't have an application that you need, it might be a constant source of frustration for you as you try to use that distro on a daily basis.

For example, Ubuntu and Fedora. Ubuntu has much larger software repositories and more third-party support. If you plan on using your desktop for daily tasks and multimedia, this would definitely give Ubuntu the point.

Some distributions, like Debian, don't come with free software and package it in a separate repository. Again, this is something else to consider.

You are going to be looking at and interacting with your desktop environment every day. It is important to have something that you are comfortable with. If you have never used Linux before, something like GNOME might be intimidating, since it is nothing like a Windows or Mac desktop. Cinnamon, on the other hand, might feel like home right away. That is a major difference between Ubuntu and Linux Mint. Ubuntu ships with GNOME by default, while Mint tries to be a bit friendlier and gives you its own Cinnamon desktop.

There are also alternative desktops and different choices available within the same distribution. More advanced DIY distributions like Arch Linux and Gentoo don't have a default desktop environment at all. In fact, they don't come with a desktop environment at all. They expect you to install and set up everything by yourself. On the bright side, they also let you choose from just about any environment imaginable.

Desktop environments are also important because they usually dictate what tools come with your installation. OpenSUSE, for example, is based around KDE Plasma. Plasma has a strong set of tools available, and OpenSUSE is tested and engineered for those tools to perform flawlessly.

It would not be so great to have a desktop computer that can't update to new applications with great features because of some reasons. That's why you also need to look at how frequently your distribution releases a new version.

It gets tricky here because there is a nice middle ground that you want to reach. Running all the latest software all the time can cause things to break and that is so bad because you lose time, effort and nerves. Distributions like Arch Linux have got a bad reputation for this sort of thing, since they always come with the latest and not always greatest.

Some distributions, like OpenSUSE, Tumbleweed, SolusOS, Arch Linux, and Gentoo don't have designated versions. They update their software as its released. That doesn't necessarily mean that it is new all the time. It just means that there will never be a hard barrier to getting new software.

Some distributions that usually sit in the middle ground between outdated and bleeding edge are Ubuntu, Linux Mint, SolusOS, OpenSUSE, Debian, and ElementaryOS.

You can't overlook a distribution's community. That community consists of the people you are going to turn to when something goes wrong. Something will go wrong somewhere along the line. The Ubuntu community is massive, and it is used to helping Linux beginners to get their bearings in the new computer's world. Compare that with the Arch Linux community that expects a certain level of skill and expertise from Arch users to install and make this distribution work stable.

The community is also responsible for packaging software outside the default distribution repositories. Again, Ubuntu dictates popularity and has a huge asset here. Whenever someone supports Linux, they package for Ubuntu. Other communities are also known for packaging new software worthwhile as well. Arch Linux's repository is filled with software that the community packages and maintains for Arch.

When you are selecting a distribution for your servers the concerns are very different from a desktop. You need a system that will literally never fail. When it does and fail, you need a way to get it back running as fast as possible.

Servers need to serve, so you also need to consider which software is available for your server. Running a long term support distribution might seem like a great idea until the web application you developed won't run because of all the software in the repositories is terribly outdated.

It might seem like you need to strike a balance here, and that may be the solution in some cases, but this is more an issue of what the server's role will actually be. A web server should lean towards flexibility. Web technologies are rapidly evolving, and you don't want to find yourself custom compiling everything just to get your web app running.

On the other hand, it might not be the worst thing if your email server is a bit outdated but literally never changes. Email servers are notoriously difficult to configure, and it's usually better if they remain as secure and stable as possible.

Database servers can fall in that middle ground. Again, the database for a web application needs some new features to keep up with the software it is interacting with on a daily basis. On the other hand, if you're running an internal Debian for records or the database for an email server, you might want something simple and stable.

Linux distributions for the enterprise are usually the ones with impossibly long support windows that never really change. Distributions that are more general purpose usually move at a quicker pace and allow for some flexibility in your software choice.

Linux enterprise distributions:

- CentOS

- RHEL

- Debian

- Slackware

Linux flexible distributions:

- Ubuntu

- Debian

- Gentoo

When it comes to servers, repositories matter. Unlike desktops, this is not about whether or not your distribution will have the latest multimedia tools. It is more a question of whether your server will support the services that you want to deploy. For instance, if you wrote an application that takes advantage of a feature in the latest Python 3 release, but your server is geared entirely towards Python 2, you are in trouble.

There are two major factors that influence here. You need to know do your server distro comes with the software version you need and you have to know if that software is going to be updated and when. Maybe you want that server to receive the latest PHP versions to take advantage of the recent improvements. Then, you want to take a look if future versions will be back ported.

In other case, you might want the exact opposite. You might not want your database software changing features on you. Java updates can be a major issue too. It all depends on what you are hosting.

There is another factor to consider when choosing a server distribution. Do you want to purchase professional support from a corporate backer? Ubuntu and RHEL both have large corporation behind them offering support contracts. Other great server distributions like Debian and CentOS don't have available support, even though CentOS is a Red Hat product.

Debian and Ubuntu are very similar distributions, but Debian is developed by a non-profit entity with the help of volunteers. Ubuntu is owned and developed by Canonical, who officially supports its LTS releases. That different factor might be enough to switch your way to the other.

It is also important to consider hardware compatibility in this equation too. Canonical and Red Hat both work with hardware vendors to ensure that they fully support your hardware. Whether you like it or not, no one's testing Gentoo for hardware compatibility.

Here is no the best distribution and there isn't a single magic answer to this question. It's a choice that you need to make based on your needs and your personal preferences.

Chapter 7: Managing Hardware and installing additional Software

Hardware management for Linux software requires a particular skillset. Linux software requires hardware to be useful and managing that hardware on its own skillset.

Device files are also known as device special files. Device files are employed to provide the operating system and users an interface to the devices that they represent. All Linux device files are located in the /dev directory, which is an integral part of the root (/) file system because these device files must be available to the operating system during the boot process.

One of the most important things you should know about these device files is that they are most definitely not device drivers. They are more accurately described as portals to the device drivers. Data is passed from an application or the operating system to the device file which then passes it to the device driver which then sends it to the physical device. The reverse data path is also used, from the physical device through the device driver, the device file and then to an application or another device.

Device files can be classified in at least two ways. The first and most commonly used classification is that of the data stream commonly associated with the device. For example, the teletype and serial devices are considered to be character based because the data stream is transferred and handled one character or byte at a time. Block type devices such as hard drives transfer data in blocks, typically a multiple of 256 bytes.

The Linux Allocated Devices file at Kernel.org is the official registry of device types and major and minor number allocations. It can help you understand the major/minor numbers for all currently defined devices.

In the past, the device files in /dev were all created at installation time, resulting in a directory full of almost every possible device file, even though most would never be used. In the unlikely event that a new device file was needed or one was accidentally deleted and needed to be re-created, the program was available to manually create device files. All you had to know was the device major and minor numbers.

Although playing with scull and similar toys is a good introduction to the software interface of a Linux device driver, implementing a real device requires hardware. The driver is the abstraction layer between software concepts and hardware circuitry.

I/O Ports and I/O Memory

Every peripheral device is controlled by writing and reading its registers. Most of the time a device has several registers, and they are accessed at consecutive addresses, either in the memory address space or in the I/O (input and output) address space.

At the hardware level, there is no conceptual difference between memory regions and I/O regions is that both of them are accessed by asserting electrical signals on the address bus and control bus and by reading from or writing to the data bus.

While some CPU manufacturers implement a single address space in their chips, some others decided that peripheral devices are different from memory and therefore deserve a separate address space. Some processors have separate read and write electrical lines for I/O ports, and special CPU instructions to access ports.

For the same reason, Linux implements the concept of I/O ports on all computer platforms it runs on, even on platforms where the CPU implements a single address space. The implementation of port access sometimes depends on the specific make and model of the host computer.

Even if the peripheral bus has a separate address space for I/O ports, not all devices map their registers to I/O ports. This I/O memory approach is generally preferred because it doesn't require use of special-purpose processor instructions. CPU i-cores access memory much more efficiently, and the compiler has much more freedom in register allocation and addressing mode selection when accessing memory.

I/O Registers and Conventional Memory

Despite the strong similarity between hardware registers and memory, a programmer accessing I/O registers must be careful to avoid being tricked by CPU optimizations that can modify the expected I/O behavior.

The main difference between I/O registers and RAM is that I/O operations have side effects, while memory operations have nothing. The only effect of a memory write is storing a value to a location, and a memory return the last value written there. Because memory access speed is so critical to CPU performance, the no side effects case has been optimized in several ways, for example values are cached and read/write instructions are reordered.

The compiler can cache data values into CPU registers without writing them to memory, and even if it stores them, both write and read operations can operate on cache memory without ever reaching physical RAM. Reordering can also happen both at compiler level and at hardware level: often a sequence of instructions can be executed more quickly if it is run in an order different from that which appears in the program text.

These optimizations are transparent when applied to conventional memory, but they can be fatal to correct I/O operations because they interfere with those side effects that are the main reason why a driver accesses I/O registers. The processor cannot anticipate a situation in which some other process depends on the order of memory access. A driver must therefore ensure that no caching is performed and no read or write reordering takes place when accessing registers: the compiler or the CPU may just try to outsmart you and reorder the operations you request; the result can be strange errors that are very difficult to debug.

The problem with hardware caching is the easiest to face. The underlying hardware is already configured to disable any hardware cache when accessing I/O.

The solution to compiler optimization and hardware reordering is to place a memory barrier between operations that must be visible to the hardware in a particular order. Linux provides four macros to cover all possible ordering needs.

Because memory barriers affect performance, they should only be used where really needed. The different types of barriers can also have different performance characteristics, so it is worthwhile to use the most specific type possible. For example, on the x86 architecture wmb() currently does nothing, since writes outside the processor are not reordered. Reads are reordered, however, so mb() will be slower than wmb().

Basics of Udev in Linux

The udev daemon, systemd-udevd communicates with the kernel and receives device uevents directly from it each time you add or remove a device from the system, or a device changes its state.

Udev is based on rules. The rules are flexible and very powerful. Every received device event is matched against the set of rules read from files located in /lib/udev/rules.d and /run/udev/rules.d.

You can write custom rules files in the /etc/udev/rules.d/ directory to process a device. Note that rules files in this directory have the highest priority.

To create a device node file, udev needs to identify a device using certain attributes such as the label, serial number, its major and minor number used, bus device number and so much more. This information is exported by the sysfs file system.

Whenever you connect a device to the system, the kernel detects and initializes it, and a directory with the device name is created under /sys/ directory which stores the device attributes. The main configuration file for udev is /etc/udev/udev.conf, and to control the runtime behavior the udev daemon, you can use the udevadm utility.

Udev is a remarkable device manager that provides a dynamic way of setting up device nodes in the /dev directory. It ensures that devices are configured as soon as they are plugged in and discovered. It propagates information about a processed device or changes to its state, to user space.

Linux device driver

One of the most daunting challenges for people switching from a familiar Windows or Mac OS system to Linux is installing and configuring a driver. This is understandable, as Windows and MacOS have mechanisms that make this process user-friendly. For example, when you plug in a new piece of hardware, Windows automatically detects it and shows a pop-up window asking if you want to continue with the driver's installation. You can also download a driver from the internet, just double-click it to run a wizard or import the driver through Device Manager.

This process is not as easy on a Linux operating system. For one reason, Linux is an open source operating system, so there are hundreds of Linux distribution variations. This means that it is impossible to create one how-to guide that works for all Linux distributions. Each Linux operating system handles the driver installation process a different way.

Second, most default Linux drivers are open source and integrated into the system, which makes installing any drivers that are not included quite complicated, even though most hardware devices can be automatically detected.

Third, license policies vary among the different Linux distributions. For example, Fedora prohibits including drivers that are proprietary and legally encumbered. Ubuntu asks users to avoid using proprietary or closed hardware too.

If you are new to Linux and coming from the Windows or MacOS world, you will be glad to know that Linux offers ways to see whether a driver is available through wizard programs. Ubuntu offers the Additional Drivers option. Other Linux distributions provide helper programs, like Package Manager for GNOME, that you can check for available drivers.

What if you can't find a driver through your nice user interface application? Or you only have access through the shell with no graphic interface whatsoever? Maybe you've even decided to expand your skills by using a console. You have two options: to use a repository or to download, compile, and build it yourself.

If you choose to use a repository, this is similar to the homebrew command in MacOS. By using yum, dnf, apt-get, etc., you're basically adding a repository and updating the package cache.

If you choose the second way, this usually involves downloading a package directly from a website or using the wget command and running the configuration file and Make file to install it. This is beyond the scope of this theme, but you should be able to find online guides if you choose to go this route.

Chapter 8: How to manage Linux running processes

A process refers to a program in execution. It is a running instance of a program. This is made up of the program instruction, data read from files, other programs or any input from a system user.

There are fundamentally two types of processes in Linux: Foreground processes and background processes.

Foreground processes or interactive processes are initialized and controlled through a terminal session. In other words, there has to be a user connected to the system to start any process. They haven't started automatically as part of the system functions or services.

Background processes or automatic processes are processes that are not connected to a terminal or in details they don't expect any user input.

Daemons

Daemos are special types of background processes that start at system startup and keep running forever as a service. They don't stop. They are started as system tasks, spontaneously. However, they can be controlled by a user via the unit process.

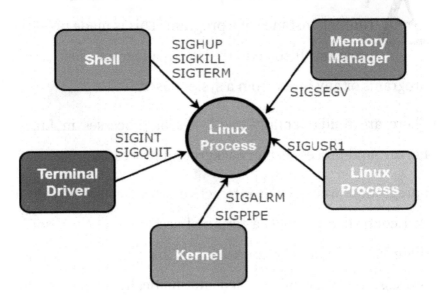

A new process is normally created when an existing process makes a copy of itself in the memory. The child process will have the same environment as its parent, but only the process ID number is different.

There are two conventional ways used for creating a new process in Linux: Using The System() function and using fork() and exec() function.

The System() Function is a method that is relatively simple. It is inefficient and has significantly certain security risks.

Fork() and Exec() Function are the techniques with a little advance but offers greater flexibility, speed and security.

Because Linux is a multi-user system, meaning different users can be running various programs on the system, each running instance of a program must be identified individually by the kernel.

A program is identified by its process ID (PID) as well as it is parent processes ID (PPID), where the processes can further be categorized into: Parent processes and Child processes.

Parent processes are processes that create other processes during the program run-time.

Child processes are processes that are created by other processes during the progtam run-time.

Init process is the mother (parent) of all processes on the system and it is the first program that is executed when the Linux system boots up. It manages all other processes on the system. It is started by the kernel itself so, in principle it does not have a parent process.

The init process always has process ID. It functions as an adoptive parent for all orphaned processes.

To find the process ID and parent process ID of the current shell, see the example below:

```
[root@tecmint ~]# echo $$
2109
[root@tecmint ~]# echo $PPID
2106
[root@tecmint ~]#
```

Once you run a command it will start with a process in the system. You can start a foreground (interactive) process as follows. It will be connected to the terminal and a user can send input in it.

```
[root@tecmint ~]# cloudcmd
url: http://localhost:8000/
```

During execution, a process changes from one state to another depending on its environment. In Linux, a process has the following possible states:

Running, where it is the current process in the system or it is ready to run

Waiting, the state where, the process is waiting for an event to occur or for a system resource. Additionally, the kernel is also different for two types of waiting processes.

The interruptible waiting processes can be interrupted by signals and non-stop waiting processes are waiting directly on hardware conditions and cannot be interrupted by any signal.

Stopped is the state where a process has been stopped, usually by receiving a signal. For instance, a process that is being debugged.

Zombie is a state where a process is dead and it has been halted but it still has an entry in the process table.

There are several Linux tools for viewing running processes on the system, the two traditional and well known are ps and top commands.

ps Command displays information about a selection of the active processes on the system. Here is a picture for example:

```
[root@tecmint ~]# ps
  PID TTY          TIME CMD
 2109 pts/0    00:00:00 bash
 2200 pts/0    00:00:01 node
 2321 pts/0    00:00:00 ps
[root@tecmint ~]# ps -e | head
  PID TTY          TIME CMD
    1 ?        00:00:01 systemd
    2 ?        00:00:00 kthreadd
    3 ?        00:00:00 ksoftirqd/0
    5 ?        00:00:00 kworker/0:0H
    6 ?        00:00:00 kworker/u2:0
    7 ?        00:00:00 migration/0
    8 ?        00:00:00 rcu_bh
    9 ?        00:00:00 rcuob/0
   10 ?        00:00:00 rcu_sched
[root@tecmint ~]# 
```

top (System Monitoring Tool) is a powerful tool that offers you a dynamic real-time view of a running system. Example:

```
[root@tecmint ~]# ps
  PID TTY          TIME CMD
 2109 pts/0    00:00:00 bash
 2200 pts/0    00:00:01 node
 2321 pts/0    00:00:00 ps
[root@tecmint ~]# ps -e | head
  PID TTY          TIME CMD
    1 ?        00:00:01 systemd
    2 ?        00:00:00 kthreadd
    3 ?        00:00:00 ksoftirqd/0
    5 ?        00:00:00 kworker/0:0H
    6 ?        00:00:00 kworker/u2:0
    7 ?        00:00:00 migration/0
    8 ?        00:00:00 rcu_bh
    9 ?        00:00:00 rcuob/0
   10 ?        00:00:00 rcu_sched
[root@tecmint ~]# 
```

glances (System Monitoring Tool) is a relatively new system monitoring tool with advanced features.

```
     tecmint (CentOS Linux 7.0.1406 64bit / Linux 3.10.0-123.el7.x86_64)     Uptime: 0:52:45

CPU         0.0%   Load   1-core    Mem    26.0%  active:    369M   Swap      0.0%
user:       0.0%   1 min:   0.19    total:  994M  inactive:  377M   total:  2.70G
system:     0.0%   5 min:   0.14    used:   258M  buffers:  51.8M   used:       0
idle:     100.0%   15 min:  0.14    free:   736M  cached:    551M   free:   2.70G

Network     Rx/s    Tx/s   Tasks    81 (107 thr),  1 run,  80 slp,  0 oth
enp0s3      176b    720b
enp0s8      160b    376b    VIRT    RES  _CPU%  MEM%   PID USER      NAME
lo            0b      0b    229M    14M   2.9   1.4   2275 root      glances
                           142M     5M   0.3   0.5   2106 root      sshd: root@pts/0
Disk I/O    In/s   Out/s    45M     6M   0.0   0.6      1 root      systemd
sda1           0      0      0       0   0.0   0.0      2 root      kthreadd
sda2           0      0      0       0   0.0   0.0      3 root      ksoftirqd/0
sr0            0      0      0       0   0.0   0.0      5 root      kworker/0:0H
                                   0       0   0.0   0.0      6 root      kworker/u2:0
Mount       Used   Total    0       0   0.0   0.0      7 root      migration/0
/           3.22G  28.7G    0       0   0.0   0.0      8 root      rcu_bh
/run        6.59M   497M    0       0   0.0   0.0      9 root      rcuob/0
_/user/0       0   99.4M    0       0   0.0   0.0     10 root      rcu_sched
_er/1003       0   99.4M    0       0   0.0   0.0     11 root      rcuos/0
_selinux       0      0      0       0   0.0   0.0     12 root      watchdog/0
                                   0       0   0.0   0.0     13 root      khelper

Press 'h' for help                                              2017-03-28 10:06:10
```

Linux also has some commands for controlling processes such as kill, pkill, pgrep and killall, here are a few basic examples of how to use them.

```
[root@tecmint ~]# pgrep -u tecmint top
2308
[root@tecmint ~]#
[root@tecmint ~]# kill 2308
[root@tecmint ~]#
[root@tecmint ~]# pgrep -u tecmint top
[root@tecmint ~]#
[root@tecmint ~]# pgrep -u tecmint glances
2311
[root@tecmint ~]#
[root@tecmint ~]# pkill glances
[root@tecmint ~]#
[root@tecmint ~]# pgrep -u tecmint glances
[root@tecmint ~]#
[root@tecmint ~]#
```

The fundamental way of controlling processes in Linux is by sending signals to them. There are multiple signals that you can send to a process, for example:

```
[root@tecmint ~]# kill -l
 1) SIGHUP        2) SIGINT       3) SIGQUIT      4) SIGILL       5) SIGTRAP
 6) SIGABRT       7) SIGBUS       8) SIGFPE       9) SIGKILL     10) SIGUSR1
11) SIGSEGV      12) SIGUSR2     13) SIGPIPE     14) SIGALRM     15) SIGTERM
16) SIGSTKFLT    17) SIGCHLD     18) SIGCONT     19) SIGSTOP     20) SIGTSTP
21) SIGTTIN      22) SIGTTOU     23) SIGURG      24) SIGXCPU     25) SIGXFSZ
26) SIGVTALRM    27) SIGPROF     28) SIGWINCH    29) SIGIO       30) SIGPWR
31) SIGSYS       34) SIGRTMIN    35) SIGRTMIN+1  36) SIGRTMIN+2  37) SIGRTMIN+3
38) SIGRTMIN+4   39) SIGRTMIN+5  40) SIGRTMIN+6  41) SIGRTMIN+7  42) SIGRTMIN+8
43) SIGRTMIN+9   44) SIGRTMIN+10 45) SIGRTMIN+11 46) SIGRTMIN+12 47) SIGRTMIN+13
48) SIGRTMIN+14  49) SIGRTMIN+15 50) SIGRTMAX-14 51) SIGRTMAX-13 52) SIGRTMAX-12
53) SIGRTMAX-11  54) SIGRTMAX-10 55) SIGRTMAX-9  56) SIGRTMAX-8  57) SIGRTMAX-7
58) SIGRTMAX-6   59) SIGRTMAX-5  60) SIGRTMAX-4  61) SIGRTMAX-3  62) SIGRTMAX-2
63) SIGRTMAX-1   64) SIGRTMAX
[root@tecmint ~]#
```

To send a signal to a process, you need to use the kill, pkill or pgrep commands. But programs can only respond to signals if they are programmed to recognize those signals.

The most signals are for internal use by the system or for programmers when they write code. The following are signals which are useful to a system user:

SIGHUP 1 is a signal to send a process when its controlling terminal is closed.

SIGINT 2 is a signal that is sent to a process by its controlling terminal when a user interrupts the process by pressing Ctrl+C from the keyboard.

SIGQUIT 3 is a signal that is sent to a process if the user sends a quit signal by pressing Ctrl+D from the keyboard.

SIGKILL 9 is a signal that immediately terminates a process and the process will not perform any cleaning/deleting operations.

SIGTERM 15 is a signal that represent a program termination signal.

SIGTSTP 20 is a sognal that is sent to a process by its controlling terminal to request it to stop and initiated by the user pressing Ctrl+Z.

On the Linux operating system, all active processes have a priority and certain nice value. Processes with higher priority will normally get more CPU time than lower priority processes.

Chapter 9: Using the Linux command line

During the starting years of the computer industry, one of the early operating systems was called Unix. It was designed to run as a multi-user system on mainframe computers, with users connecting remotely by individual terminals. These terminals were realy basic by modern standards with just a keyboard and screen, with no power to run programs. Instead they would just send keystrokes to the server and display any data they received on the screen. There was no fancy graphics, not even any choice of color. Everything was sent as a text and received as a text. Obviously, any programs that ran on the mainframe had to produce text as an output and accept text as an input.

Compared with graphics, text is very light on resources. Even on machines from the 1970s, running hundreds of terminals across glacially slow network connections, users were still able to interact with programs quickly and efficiently. The commands were also kept to reduce the number of keystrokes needed, speeding up people's use of the terminal and much more. This speed and efficiency is one of the reasons why this text interface is still widely used today.

When you log in into a Unix mainframe via a terminal users, you will still had to manage the sort of file management tasks that you might now perform with a couple of windows. Whether creating files, renaming them, putting them into sub-directories or moving them around on disk, users in the 70s could do everything entirely with a textual interface.

Each of these tasks required its own program or command. One to change directories (cd), another to list their contents (ls), a third to rename or move files (mv) and so on. In order to coordinate the execution of each of these programs, the user would connect to one single master program that could then be used to launch any of the others. By wrapping the user's commands this "shell" program could provide common capabilities to any of them, such as the ability to pass data from one command straight into another or to use special wildcard characters to work with lots of similar named files at once.

Users could even write simple code which could be used to automate long series of shell commands in order to make complex tasks easier. The original Unix shell program was just called 'sh' but it has been extended over the years, so on a modern Linux system you are most likely to be using a shell called bash.

Linux is a sort-of-descendent of Unix. The core part of Linux is designed to behave similarly to a Unix system, such as the old shells and other text-based programs run on quite happily. In theory, you could even hook up one of those old 1970s terminals to a modern Linux box and access the shell through that. These days it is far more common to use a software terminal as old Unix-style text interface, but running in a window alongside your graphical programs.

Terminal

On your chosen Linux distribution, you can find a launcher for the terminal by clicking on the Activities item at the top left corner of the screen and type the first few letters of "terminal", "command", "prompt" or "shell". The developers have set up the launcher with all the most common synonyms, so you should have no problems finding it.

Other versions of Linux, or other Linux distros, will have a terminal launcher located in the same place as your other application launchers. It might be hidde in a submenu or you might have to search for it from within your launcher.

If you can't find a launcher, or if you just want a faster way to bring up the terminal, most Linux systems use the same default keyboard shortcut to start it, with pressing Ctrl-Alt-T.

However if you launched your terminal, you should end up with a rather dull looking window with an odd bit of text at the top.

Depending on your Linux operating system, the colors may not be the same and the text will likely say something different, but the general layout of a window with a large text area should be similar.

You should see a directory path printed out probably something like: /home/YOUR_USERNAME.

```
                                    mark@linux-desktop: ~

 File  Edit  View  Search  Terminal  Help
mark@linux-desktop:~$ pwd
/home/mark
mark@linux-desktop:~$
```

There are a couple of basics to understand here, before you get into the detail of what the command actually did.

First, when you type a command it appears on the same line as the odd text. That text is there to tell you the computer is ready to accept a command. It is the computer's way of prompting you. They are just different ways of asking you to open a terminal to get to a shell.

On the subject of synonyms, another way of looking at the prompt is to say that there is a line in the terminal into which you type commands. Again, if you see a mention of "command line" it is just another way of talking about a shell running in a terminal.

The second thing is that when you run a command, any output it produces will usually be printed directly in the terminal when you will be shown another prompt once it is finished. Some commands can output a lot of text while others will operate silently and won't output anything at the end of a day. Don't be alarmed if you run a command and another prompt immediately appears because that usually means the command succeeded.

The pwd is a short of 'print working directory'. All it does is print out the shell's current working directory, but what is a working directory?

One important concept to understand this is that the shell has a notion of a default location in which any file operations will take place. This is its working directory. If you try to create new files or directories, view existing files or even delete them, the shell will assume you are looking for them in the current working directory unless you take steps to specify otherwise. So it is quite important to keep an idea of what directory the shell is "in" at any given time. If you are in any doubt, the pwd command will tell you exactly what the current working directory is.

Now the working directory is "/". If you are coming from a Windows background you are probably used to each drive having its own letter, with your main hard drive typically being "C:". Unix-like systems don't split up the drives like that. Instead they have a single unified file system, and individual drives can be attached to whatever location in the file system makes most sense. The "/" directory often referred to the root directory which is the base of that unified file system. From there, everything else branches out to form a tree of directories and sub-directories.

The place you end up depends on your current working directory. Consider trying to 'cd' into the "etc" folder. If you are already in the root directory, that will work fine. But what if you are in your home directory?

You will see an error saying "No such file or directory" before you even get to run the last pwd. Changing directory by specifying the directory name will have different effects depending on where you start from. The path only makes sense relative to your working directory.

No matter what your current working directory is, they will have the same effect. The first is when you run 'cd' on its own to go straight to your home directory.

The second is when you used cd / to switch to the root directory. In fact, any path that starts with a forward / is an absolute path. You can think of it as saying "switch to the root directory, then follow the route from there". That gives you a much easier way to switch to the 'etc' directory, no matter where we currently are in the file system.

Folders and files

To avoid accidentally trampling over any of your real files, we are going to start by creating a new directory away from your home folder, which will serve as a safer environment.

Without the forward slash at the start the mkdir command, would try to find a tmp directory inside the current working directory, then try to create a tutorial directory inside that. If it couldn't find a tmp directory, the command would fail.

In case you hadn't guessed, mkdir is short for 'make directory'. For example: mkdir dir1 dir2 dir3...

There's something a little different about that command. So far, we have only seen commands that work on their own cd, pwd or that have a single item afterwards. But this time we have added three things after the mkdir command. Those things are referred to as parameters or arguments, and different commands can accept different numbers of arguments. The mkdir command expects at least one argument, whereas the cd command can work with zero or one, but no more. If you followed the last few commands, your terminal should be looking something like this picture example:

```
                        mark@linux-desktop: /tmp/tutorial
 File  Edit  View  Search  Terminal  Help
mark@linux-desktop:~$ mkdir /tmp/tutorial
mark@linux-desktop:~$ cd /tmp/tutorial
mark@linux-desktop:/tmp/tutorial$ mkdir dir1 dir2 dir3
mark@linux-desktop:/tmp/tutorial$ mkdir
mkdir: missing operand
Try 'mkdir --help' for more information.
mark@linux-desktop:/tmp/tutorial$ cd /etc ~/Desktop
bash: cd: too many arguments
mark@linux-desktop:/tmp/tutorial$ ls
dir1  dir2  dir3
mark@linux-desktop:/tmp/tutorial$ █
```

Our demonstration folder is starting to look rather full of directories, but is somewhat lacking in files. Let's remedy that by redirecting the output from a command so that, instead of being printed to the screen, it ends up in a new file.

Suppose we wanted to capture the output of that command as a text file that we can look at or manipulate further. All we need to do is to add the greater-than character (">") to the end of the command line, followed by the name of the file: ls > output.txt

This time, there is nothing printed to the screen, because the output is being redirected to our file instead. If you just run ls on its own you should see that the output.txt file has been created. We can use the cat command: cat output.txt

Generally you should try to avoid creating files and folders whose name only varies by case. Not only will it help to avoid confusion, but it will also prevent problems when working with different operating systems. Windows, for example, is case-insensitive, so it would treat all three of the file names above as being a single file, potentially causing data loss or other problems.

You might be tempted to just hit the Caps Lock key and use upper case for all your file names. But the vast majority of shell commands are lower case, so you would end up frequently having to turn it on and off as you type. Most seasoned command line users tend to stick primarily to lower case names for their files and directories so that they rarely have to worry about file name clashes, or which case to use for each letter in the name.

Manipulating with files

Now that we have got a few files, let's take a look at the sort of day-to-day tasks you might need to perform on them. In practice you will still most likely use a graphical program when you want to move, rename or delete one or two files, but knowing how to do this using the command line can be useful for bulk changes, or when the files are spread amongst different folders.

Let's start by putting our combined.txt file into our dir1 directory, using the mv command: mv combined.txt dir1

You can confirm that the job has been done by using ls to see that it is missing from the working directory, then cd dir1 to change into dir1, ls to see that it is in there to move the working directory back again. Or you could save a lot of typing by passing a path directly to the ls command to get straight to the confirmation you are looking for: ls dir1

The mv command also lets us move more than one file at a time. If you pass more than two arguments, the last one is taken to be the destination directory and the others are considered to be files to move.

This is a powerful property of the command line: no matter where in the file system you are, it's still possible to operate on files and folders in totally different locations.

This also works on directories, giving us a way to sort out those difficult ones with spaces in the name that we created earlier. To avoid re-typing each command after the first, use the Up Arrow to pull up the previous command in the history. You can then edit the command before you run it by moving the cursor left and right with the arrow keys, and removing the character to the left with Backspace or the one the cursor is on with Delete. Finally, type the new character in place, and press Enter or Return to run the command once you're finished. Make sure you change both appearances of the number in each of these lines.

Deleting files and folders

Now we know how to move, copy and rename files and directories. Given that these are just test files, however, perhaps we don't really need three different copies of combined.txt after all. Here is an example:

rm dir4/dir5/dir6/combined.txt combined_backup.txt

Perhaps we should remove some of those excess directories as well: rm folder_*

```
mark@linux-desktop: /tmp/tutorial
File Edit View Search Terminal Help
mark@linux-desktop:/tmp/tutorial$ mv "folder 1" folder_1
mark@linux-desktop:/tmp/tutorial$ mv "folder 2" folder_2
mark@linux-desktop:/tmp/tutorial$ mv "folder 3" folder_3
mark@linux-desktop:/tmp/tutorial$ mv "folder 4" folder_4
mark@linux-desktop:/tmp/tutorial$ mv "folder 5" folder_5
mark@linux-desktop:/tmp/tutorial$ mv "folder 6" folder_6
mark@linux-desktop:/tmp/tutorial$ ls
another           dir1    folder      folder_3  folder_6
combined_backup.txt dir2  folder_1   folder_4  output.txt
combined.txt       dir4   folder_2   folder_5
mark@linux-desktop:/tmp/tutorial$ rm dir4/dir5/dir6/combined.txt combined_backup
.txt
mark@linux-desktop:/tmp/tutorial$ rm folder_*
rm: cannot remove 'folder_1': Is a directory
rm: cannot remove 'folder_2': Is a directory
rm: cannot remove 'folder_3': Is a directory
rm: cannot remove 'folder_4': Is a directory
rm: cannot remove 'folder_5': Is a directory
rm: cannot remove 'folder_6': Is a directory
mark@linux-desktop:/tmp/tutorial$
```

The addition of options to our rm or rmdir commands will let us perform dangerous actions without the aid of a safety net! In the case of rmdir we can add a -p switch to tell it to also remove the parent directories. Think of it as the counterpoint to mkdir -p. So if you were to run rmdir -p dir1/dir2/dir3 it would first delete dir3, then dir2, then finally delete dir1. It still follows the normal rmdir rules of only deleting empty directories though, so if there was also a file in dir1, for example, only dir3 and dir2 would get removed.

A more common approach, when you're really, really, really sure you want to delete a whole directory and anything within it, is to tell rm to work recursively by using the -r switch in which case it will happily delete folders as well as files.

Unlike graphical interfaces, rm doesn't move files to a folder called "trash" or similar. Instead it deletes them totally, utterly and irrevocably. You need to be careful with the parameters you use with rm to make sure you are only deleting the file you intend to.

You should take particular care when using wildcards, as it is easy to accidentally delete more files than you intended. If you are at all uncertain use the -i option to rm, which will prompt you to confirm the deletion of each file so, enter Y to delete it, N to keep it and press Ctrl + C to stop the operation entirely.

A bit of pipes and 'plumbing'

Today's computers and smartphones have the sort of graphical and audio capabilities that the 70s terminal users couldn't even begin to imagine. Yet still text prevails as a means to organize and categorize files. Whether it is the file name itself, GPS coordinates embedded in photos you take on your phone or the metadata stored in an audio file, text still plays a vital role in every aspect of computing. It is a fortune for us that the Linux command line includes some powerful tools for manipulating text content, and ways to join those tools together to create something more capable still.

The wc or word count command can tell us that, using the -l switch to tell it we only want the line count. Here is the example of that command: wc -l combined.txt

Similarly, if you wanted to know how many files and folders are in your home directory, and then tidy up after yourself, you need to use this example:

- ls ~ > file_list.txt

- wc -l file_list.txt

- rm file_list.txt

That method works, but creating a temporary file to hold the output from ls only to delete it two lines later seems a little excessive. Fortunately, the Unix command line provides a shortcut that avoids you having to create a temporary file, by taking the output from one command and feeding it directly in as the input to another command. It is like you have connected a pipe between one command's output and the next command's input so this process is actually referred to as piping the data from one command to another. Here is an example of ls command piped into wc: ls ~ | wc -l

Notice that there is no temporary file created and no file name needed, pipes operate entirely in memory, and most Unix command line tools will expect to receive input from a pipe if you don't specify a file for them to work on. Looking at the line above, you can see that it is two commands, ls and wc -l separated by a vertical bar character ("|"). This process of piping one command into another is so commonly used that the character itself is often referred to as the pipe character, so if you see that term you now know it just means the vertical bar.

Going back to our own files, we know how to get the number of lines in combined.txt, but given that it was created by concatenating the same files multiple times. Unix has a command 'uniq' that will only output unique lines in the file. We need to cat the file out and pipe it through uniq command. But all we want is a line count, so we need to use wc as well. Fortunately the command line doesn't limit you to a single pipe at a time, so we can continue to chain as many commands as we need.

The command example: cat combined.txt | uniq | wc -l

That line probably resulted in a count that is pretty close to the total number of lines in the file, if not exactly the same. Lop off the last pipe to see the output of the command for a better idea of what is happening. If your file is very long, you might want to pipe it through less to make it easier to inspect.

The command example: cat combined.txt | uniq | less

It appears that very few of our duplicate lines are being removed. Most command line tools come with a brief instruction manual, accessed through the man command. The output is automatically piped through your pager, which will typically be less, so you can move back and forth through the output, then press q when you're finished.

The command example: man uniq

The picture example:

```
                          mark@linux-desktop: /tmp/tutorial              ● ● ✕
 File  Edit  View  Search  Terminal  Help
 UNIQ(1)                           User Commands                         UNIQ(1)

 NAME
        uniq - report or omit repeated lines

 SYNOPSIS
        uniq [OPTION]... [INPUT [OUTPUT]]

 DESCRIPTION
        Filter  adjacent matching lines from INPUT (or standard input), writing
        to OUTPUT (or standard output).

        With no options, matching lines are merged to the first occurrence.

        Mandatory arguments to long options are  mandatory  for  short  options
        too.

        -c, --count
               prefix lines by the number of occurrences
 Manual page uniq(1) line 1 (press h for help or q to quit)
```

Because this type of documentation is accessed via the man command, you will hear it referred to 'man page', as in "check the man page for more details. They are often highly technical, but you can usually skip most of the content and just look for the details of the option or argument you are using.

The 'uniq' man page is a typical example in that it starts with a brief one-line description of the command, moves on to a synopsis of how to use it, then has a detailed description of each option or parameter. While man pages are invaluable, they can also be in penetrable. They are best used when you need a reminder of a particular switch or parameter, rather than as a general resource for learning how to use the command line. However, the first line of the descriotion section for 'man uniq' does answer the question why the duplicated lines haven't been removed. It only works on adjacent matching lines.

The question then is how to rearrange the lines in our file so that duplicate entries are on adjacent lines. If we were to sort the contents of the file alphabetically, that would do the trick. Unix offers a sort command to do exactly that. A quick check of man sort shows that we can pass a file name directly to the command. Here is the example of the command: sort combined.txt | less

You should be able to see that the lines have been reordered and it is now suitable for piping straight into 'uniq' command. We can finally complete our task of counting the unique lines in the file. Here is the command example: sort combined.txt | uniq | wc-l

Most Linux command line tools include a 'man page'. Try taking a brief look at the pages for some of the commands you have already encountered. There's even a man page for the man program itself, which is accessed using 'man man', of course.

The command line and the superuser (su) command

One good reason for learning some command line basics is that instructions online will often do a favor for the use of shell commands over a graphical interface. Where those instructions require changes to your machine that go beyond modifying a few files in your home directory, you will be sure faced with commands that need to be run as the machine's administrator. Before you start running arbitrary commands you find in some dark corner of the internet, it is worth understanding the implications of running as an administrator, and how to spot those instructions that require it, so you can better gauge whether they are safe to run or not.

The superuser is, as the name suggests, a user with super powers. In older systems it was a real user, with a real username that you could log in as if you had the password. As for those super powers, root can modify or delete any file in any directory on the system, regardless of who owns them. Root can rewrite firewall rules or start network services that could potentially open the machine up to an attack and also can shut down the machine even if other people are still using it. In short, root can do anything, skipping easily round the safeguards that are usually put in place to stop users from overstepping their bounds.

A person logged in as a root is just as capable of making mistakes as anyone else. The annals of computing history are filled with tales of a mistyped command deleting the entire file system or killing a vital server. There is the possibility of a malicious attack. If a user is logged in as root and leaves their desk then it is not too tricky for a disgruntled colleague to hop on their computer and make a mess. Despite that, human nature being what it is, many administrators over the years have been guilty of using root as their main or only account.

In an effort to reduce these problems, many Linux distributions started to encourage the use of the 'su' command. This is variously described as being short for 'superuser' or 'switch user' and allows you to change to another user on the machine without having to log out and in again. When this is used with no arguments, it assumes you want to change to the root, but you can pass a username to it in order to switch to a specific user account. By encouraging the use of 'su' command, the aim was to persuade administrators to spend most of their time using a normal account, only switch to the superuser account when they needed to, and then use the logout command as soon as possible to return to their user-level account.

By the taking less amount of time spent logged in as root, the use of su reduces the window of opportunity in which to make a terrible mistake. Despite that, human nature being what it is, many administrators have been guilty of leaving long-running terminals open in which they have used 'su' command to switch to the root account. In that respect 'su' was only a small step forward for security.

When using su your entire terminal session is switched to the other user. Commands that don't need root access, something as mundane as pwd or ls, would be run under the auspices of the 'superuser' command, increasing the risk of a bug in the program causing major problems. Worse still, if you lose track of which user you are currently operating as, you might issue a command that is fairly benign when run as a user, but which could destroy the entire system if run as root.

Better to disable the root account entirely and then, instead of allowing long-lived terminal sessions with dangerous powers, require the user to specifically request superuser rights on a per-command basis. The key to this approach is a command called 'sudo'

The command 'sudo' is used to prefix a command that has to be run with 'superuser' privileges. A configuration file is used to define which users can use 'sudo' and which commands they can run. When running a command like this, the user is prompted for own password, which is then cached for a period of time so if they need to run multiple superuser-level commands they don't keep getting continually asked to type it in.

Assuming you are on a Linux system that uses 'sudo' and your account is configured as an administrator, try the following to see what happens when you try to access a file that is considered sensitive.

```
                    mark@linux-desktop: /tmp/tutorial

 File  Edit  View  Search  Terminal  Help
mark@linux-desktop:/tmp/tutorial$ cat /etc/shadow
cat: /etc/shadow: Permission denied
mark@linux-desktop:/tmp/tutorial$ sudo cat /etc/shadow
[sudo] password for mark:
```

If you enter your password when prompted you should see the contents of the /etc/shadow file. Now clear the terminal by running the reset command and run 'sudo' cat /etc/shadow again. This time the file will be displayed without prompting you for a password, as it's still in the cache.

For instructions targeting Ubuntu as a certin Linux distribution, a common appearance of 'sudo' is to install new software onto your system using the 'apt' or 'apt-get' commands. If the instructions require you to first add a new software repository to your system using the 'apt-add-repository' command, by editing files in /etc/apt, or by using a "PPA" (Personal Package Archive) standard repositories, which should be safe.

Once you have provided your password the 'apt' program will print out quite a few lines of text to tell you what it's doing. The tree program is only small, so it shouldn't take more than a minute or two to download and install for most users. Once you are returned to the normal command line prompt, the program is installed and ready to use.

```
                        mark@linux-desktop: /tmp/tutorial
 File  Edit  View  Search  Terminal  Help
Setting up tree (1.7.0-5) ...
Processing triggers for man-db (2.8.3-2) ...
mark@linux-desktop:/tmp/tutorial$ tree
.
├── another
├── combined.txt
├── dir1
├── dir2
│   ├── dir3
│   ├── test_1.txt
│   ├── test_2.txt
│   └── test_3.txt
├── dir4
│   └── dir5
│       └── dir6
├── folder
└── output.txt

8 directories, 5 files
mark@linux-desktop:/tmp/tutorial$
```

Going back to the command that actually installed the new it looks slightly different to those you will see so far.

The 'sudo' command, when used without any options, will assume that the first parameter is a command for it to run with superuser privileges. Any other parameters will be passed directly to the new command. This command switches all start with one or two hyphens and must immediately follow the 'sudo' command, so there can be no confusion about whether the second parameter on the line is a command or an option.

The command in this case is apt. Unlike the other commands we have seen, this is not working directly with files. Instead it expects its first parameter to be an instruction to perform with the rest of the parameters varying based on the instruction.

In this case the install command tells 'apt' that the remainder of the command line will consist of one or more package names to install from the system's software repositories. Usually this will add new software to the machine, but packages could be any collection of files that need to be installed to particular locations, such as fonts or desktop images.

You can put 'sudo' in front of any command to run it as a 'superuser', but there is rarely any need to. Even system configuration files can often be viewed as a normal user and only require root privileges if you need to edit them.

One trick with 'sudo' command is to use it to run the 'su' command. This will give you a root shell even if the root account is disabled. It can be useful when you need to run a series of commands as the 'superuser' to avoid having to prefix them all with sudo, but it opens you up to exactly the same kind of problems that were described for 'su' above. If you follow any instructions that tell you to run 'sudo su', be aware that every command after that will be running as the root user.

Linux hidden files

The hidden files are commonly used on Linux systems to store settings and configuration data and are hidden simply so, they don't clutter the view of your own files. There is nothing special about a hidden file or folder, other than it is name simply starting with a dot (".") is enough to make it disappear.

Here is the command example:

 cd /tmp/tutorial

ls

mv combined.txt .combined.txt

ls

Switch back to your home directory (cd) and try running ls without and then with the -a switch. Pipe the output through wc -l to give you a clearer idea of how many hidden files and folders have been right under your nose all this time. These files typically store your personal configuration and this is how Unix systems have always offered the capability to have system-level settings that can be overridden by individual users.

You don't need to deal with hidden files, but occasionally instructions might require you to 'cd' into .config or edit some file whose name starts with a dot. At least now you will understand what's happening, even when you can't easily see the file in your graphical tools.

We've reached the end of this tutorial, and you should be back in your home directory now. It is only polite to leave your computer in the same state that we found it in, so as a final step. Here is an example of cleaning up the hidden files:

rm -r /tmp/tutorial

ls /tmp

You can just close the window, but it is better practice to log out of the shell. You can either use the logout command or to press the Ctrl+D keyboard shortcut. If you plan to use the terminal a lot, press Ctrl+Alt+T to launch the terminal and Ctrl+D to close it will soon make it feel like a handy assistant that you can call on instantly and dismiss just as easily.

Chapter 10: Linux Applications

Being a new Linux user, sometimes you may feel your Linux system is scary and confusing if you recently have come from Windows or Mac OS. But unquestionably the Linux Environment is not like that. Here you can enjoy the freedom of using lots of amazing Best Linux software which comes free of cost mostly. Here are the best Linux software which will help the Linux users to get the latest and best Linux apps from different categories.

But the best software for Linux is subjective and depends on users need. Moreover, in the Linux world, there are lots of alternative to every software like many distros to choose from.

1. Partition Manager

There are lots of choices comes to mind when the question arises about best Linux Partition Manager. If you are a new Linux user or not comfortable with a text-based partition manager, then GUI based Gparted is the best option for you to choose. You can do almost all the task of disk partitioning using this free and open source partition manager.

2. PDF Editor

PDF is considered the best way of emailing, sharing or printing various documents. It is a well supported format across all the OS including Linux, Windows, Mac OS, Android and much more. There are many good options out there for selecting best Linux PDF Editor for every OS.

LibreOffice Draw is one of them which comes preinstalled in all the major Linux distributions. It is a free and open source

Linux pdf editor which let you fulfill the necessary task. Master PDF Editor is another one which comes with lots of features and tools for editing PDF files in Linux, but it is not a free and open source.

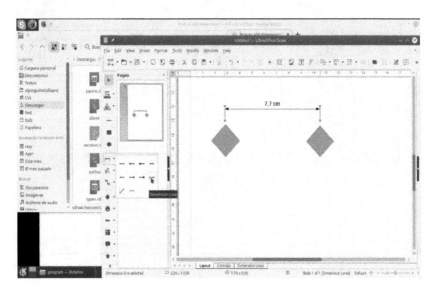

3. LaTeX Editor

In the arena of Linux, LaTeX is considered as a standard markup language. It helps the users for editing the documents to markup level. TeXmaker is one of the best LaTeX editors available out there. It is the most user-friendly LaTeX IDE for the newbie.

There are lots of best LaTeX Editor available for Linux, but it seems difficult to choose the Best LaTeX Editor for both advanced and beginner.

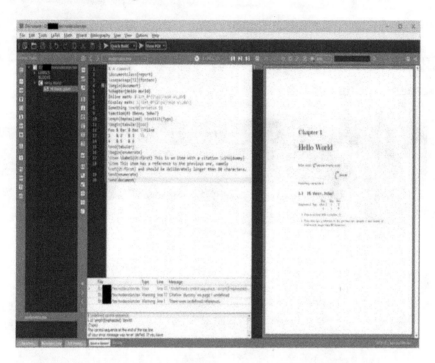

4. Screen Recorder

Screencasting is an important task for many people for many reasons including making a video tutorial, creating a presentation, compiling a how-to tutorial or do a software review or having the fun of streaming while playing pc games. Moreover now a day many users are making an earning opportunity for themselves through YouTube, Facebook video or any other video hosting sites by making many helpful how-to guide videos.

Kazam is one of the best lightweight screen recorder available for Linux desktop. It is straightforward and nifty tool for screen casting.

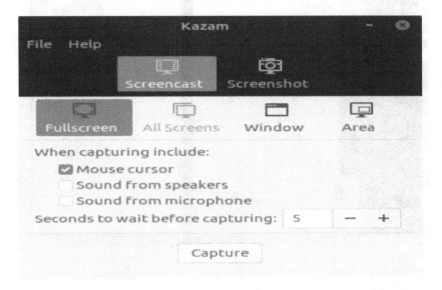

5. Torrent Client

If you are searching for something that is entirely free, open source and comes with minimum configuration, then Transmission torrent client is one of them. It supports cross-platform like Windows, Linux, Mac OS, and Unix based systems.

There are lots of favorite torrent clients available in the market. But it's challenging to find out which one comes with the best set of features.

6. FTP Client

FTP or File Transfer Protocol is one of the great and efficient ways of transferring files over a TCP based system like the internet. It helps to move a large number of computer files from one host or system to another host or system without any hassle and complexity.

FileZilla comes on top of this list of best Linux FTP Client. This FTP app is one of the best and secured FTP client for all the major platforms like Linux, Unix, Windows, and MacOS. FileZilla is a reliable and fast FTP, FTPS and SFTP client for Linux.

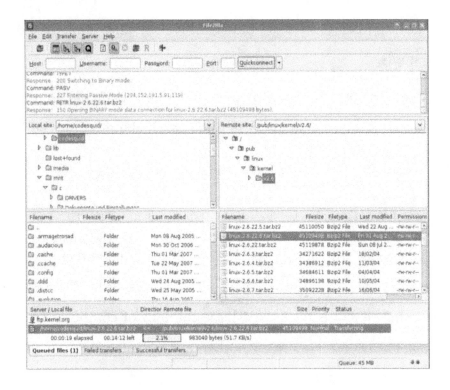

7. Backup Software

To recovers from some unexpected situations like human errors, Disk failure or RAID, Corruption of file systems we need a good backup plan.

Bacula is an Open Source Backup Software. This computer backup system can work in various networks. It is an automated task that need not require intervention from a systems administrator or computer operator. Bacula supports Linux, UNIX, and Windows backup clients.

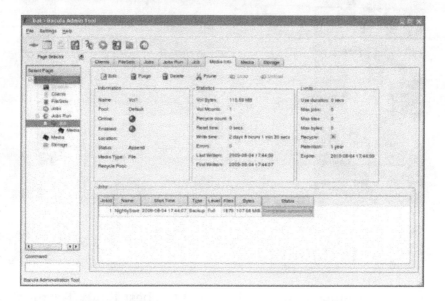

8. Note Taking App

Simplenote is the best note taking the app for Linux right now. It provides all the features that a modern and professional note-taking app must have.

Evernote is one of the best and top graded note taking apps for all the dominant OS. But Evernote doesn't provide an official client for Linux.

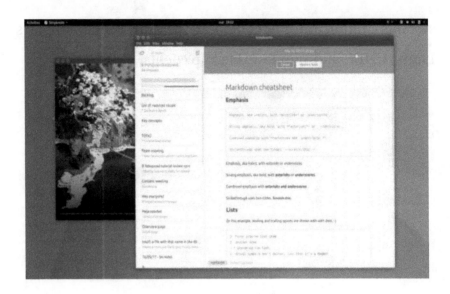

9. Terminal Emulator

Gnome Terminal emulator is one of the best Linux Terminal Emulators for Linux Gnome desktop environment. It has lots of practical and useful features that make it standalone from others.

Most of the users are satisfied with the default Terminal emulator of their Linux Distributions. But the option is always open to trying a different one and get settled with that.

10. Code Editor

Coding is great fun. You can make useful and great apps for your operating system if you can learn well how to do coding. To be a great applications developer, you have to know about all the details of coding or programming in various applications.

Atom is a Linux code editor that is smart, trendy, approachable, and yet customizable to the core. This excellent Linux text editor offers you to customize it to do anything you want.

There are various types of code editors or text editors or HTML editors for several operating systems which are available to make your coding capability easy and quick, while some of them have worked great across the OS. For creating new software in Linux, there are lots of Linux code editor available out there. Those can make you an expert Linux code developer.

11. Linux Antivirus

In the world of computer Operating System, there are always errors and problems especially intentionally made errors which we call trojan, malware, virus. Linux OS is much more efficient and secure OS but still, there are possibilities to have these problems. To decreasing this issue, security specialist has developed a Linux antivirus to detect and remove those threats before they harm the system.

In the AV-Test, Sophos is one of the best free antiviruses for Linux. It does support not only on-demand scanning but also provide real-time scanning feature.

12. Educational Software

An educational expense is always high all over the world. This expense will be more if you want to use educational software on your machine. You may be searching over the net to get the best educational software for the kids or yourself.

KDE Edu suite is not just software; it is a package of software for different user purpose. This software was started as a free educational package named as KDE educational project which now included lots of software package.

Artikulate	Blinken	Cantor
Pronunciation Trainer	Memory Enhancement Game	KDE Frontend to Mathematical Software
GCompris	KAlgebra	Kalzium
Educational suite	Graph Calculator	Periodic Table of Elements
Kanagram	KBruch	KGeography
Letter Order Game	Exercise Fractions	Geography Trainer
KHangMan	Kig	Kiten
Hangman Game	Interactive Geometry	Japanese Reference/Study Tool
KLettres	KmPlot	Kst
Learn The Alphabet	Mathematical Function Plotter	Data Viewer
KStars	KTouch	KTurtle
Desktop Planetarium	Touch Typing Tutor	Educational Programming Environment
KWordQuiz	LabPlot	Marble
Flash Card Trainer	Scientific Data Plotter	Virtual Globe
Minuet	Parley	Rocs
Music Education Software	Vocabulary Trainer	Rocs Graph Theory

13. Video Editing Software

Video editing on Linux is very easy if you find the best Video Editing Software. There is a lot of open source Video Editing Software available on Linux. You can easily customize or edit any kinds of media files with those Video Editing Software.

Open Shot video editor is an open source Video Editing Software on Ubuntu. It works well in the other distribution of Linux.

Open Shot Video Editor is very easy to install on Various Linux distribution. You can install it from the software center or use this command:

sudo add-apt-repository ppa:openshot.developers/ppa

sudo apt update

sudo apt install openshot-qt

14. Download Manager

It is obvious to have a good download manager for Linux or Ubuntu. Though all the modern browsers have default download manager, it is not good enough to handle effective downloading system. When the question comes whether a web browser can handle multiple download, pause system, torrent integration or fast download then the answer is not satisfactory.

uGet is an open source download manager for Linux which will download your files fast. This download manager can be efficiently organized and highly configurable. You can control your downloads in one central place.

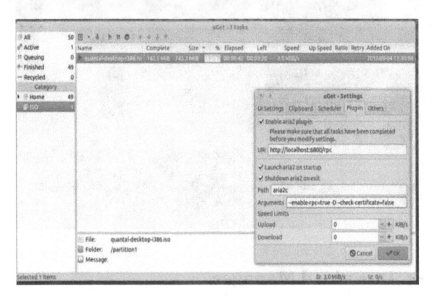

15. Video Player

VLC Media Player is one of the best and most popular Best Linux Software in the category of video players. It is an open source media player which support almost all media file types on Linux. VLC Media Player support network shares are browsing, downloading subtitles, video playlists, pop-up video, etc.

There are a lot of video players available for Linux. Those video players mainly do the same thing to play a video file. So, you need to find which video player will offer you the additional features of playing any video.

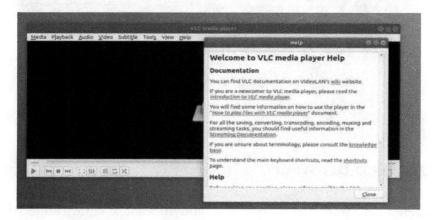

16. Google Drive Client

Google Drive offers an official client for all the dominant OS except Linux until now. As a Linux user, you have lots of ways and alternatives for using Google Drive. There are many Google Drive Linux Client software available out there that can do the work for you seamlessly.

If you think Insync Google Drive desktop client is costly, then overGrive can be an excellent choice. You can enjoy all the features and tools that Insync can offer but just for $4.99 one time payment. Over Grive supports all the major Linux desktop environments and distributions.

17. Web Browser

Generally, web browsers allow you to visit a wide range of information by accessing the online web. As there is plenty of browsing software available for Linux, undoubtedly it will puzzle you to choose the best one for your Ubuntu system.

Chromium and Google Chrome, Both the web browsers come with malware blocking that ultimately ensures personal information security. Moreover, there are lots of plugins in the chrome store which eventually let you increase the functionality of the browser in the Linux system.

18. Media Server Software

Linux Media Server software can help you to set up a cost and resource useful media server which ultimately let you watch or share or listen all the media files from a remote location on Smartphone or desktop.

Kodi is one of the best free and open source media server software available in the market. It offers an intuitive graphical user interface with lots of customization options. Kodi is an all in one entertainment software center which supports all the primary OS including Android, Linux, Windows, iOS, and MacOS.

19. Cloud Storage

OwnCloud is one of the popular and most prominent open source community driven cloud software available in the market. It let you create easy to use a personal cloud server for both home and office use. You can also have full control over your data and who can have access at all.

20. Email Client

I believe you know about Mozilla foundation and its Firefox browser which is lighting fast and patron of open source software. Thunderbird is an incredible open source and faster Linux email client from the same development house of

Firefox. It is a cross-platform, more rapid, modern web email technologies for using email services.

21. Image Editor

GIMP is an insanely popular open source Free Photo Editing Software Like Photoshop. It's a multi-platform supported software which supports various system like Windows, Linux, Mac OS X and so forth. Users can quickly complete the job with this free software.

22. Firewall Software

Iptables or Netfilter is the most popular and blazing fast open source CLI based Linux firewall. Many system administrators prefer to use it for their server protection as it plays the first line of defense of a Linux server protection.

23. VPN Client and Services

ExpressVPN is one of the best VPN for Linux, and it supports a wide range of Linux distros including Ubuntu, Debian, CentOS, Fedora, etc. This VPN service provides important Linux support and speedy performance.

24. Online Linux Terminal

Online Linux Terminal or emulator is the best way to practice or learn Linux commands without having a full-fledged Linux subsystem. There are no online Linux Terminals and bash scripts available in the market which let you run various shells, scripts, and commands to test or analyze the results. Among all of them, Codeany where is the best online Linux Terminal.

25. Linux Monitoring Tools

There are many Linux Monitoring Tools available in the market including open source software, third-party solutions, and homemade scripts run via cron. Each has its advantages and disadvantages. I have compiled a comprehensive list of Linux monitoring tools which includes all the elements of a Linux system like network, process management, server maintain etc.

26. Linux PDF Viewer

This software allows to underlines, markup, highlighting your pdf files and every user always feels the necessity of these tasks. On the other hand, the tool never allows editing, converting which can break the security of the files.

Chapter 11: The Linux Shell

The shell is a program that takes commands from the keyboard and gives them to the operating system to perform. In the old days, it was the only user interface available on a Unix system such as Linux. Nowadays, we have graphical user interfaces (GUIs) in addition to command line interfaces (CLIs) such as the shell.

On the most Linux systems, a program called "bash" acts as the shell program. Besides bash, there are other shell programs that can be installed in a Linux system, including ksh, tcsh and zsh.

A Shell provides you with an interface to the Unix system. It gathers input from you and executes programs based on that input. When a program finishes executing, it displays that program's output.

Shell is an environment in which we can run our commands, programs, and shell scripts. There are different flavors of a shell, just as there are different flavors of operating systems. Each flavor of shell has its own set of recognized commands and functions.

The prompt '$' which is called the "command prompt" is issued by the shell. While the prompt is displayed, you can type a command.

Shell reads your input after you press Enter. It determines the command you want executed by looking at the first word of your input. A word is an unbroken set of characters. Spaces and tabs separate words.

In Unix, there are two major types of Linux shell:

- Bourne shell

- C shell

Bourne shell is used for $ character which is default promt.

The Bourne Shell has original characteristics:

- Bourne shell (sh)

- Korn shell (ksh)

- Bourne Again shell (bash)

- POSIX shell (sh)

If you are using a C-type shell, the % character is the default prompt.

There are different C-type shells characteristics:

- C shell (csh)

- TENEX/TOPS C shell (tcsh)

The original Unix shell was written in the mid-1970s by Stephen R. Bourne while he was at the AT&T Bell Labs in New Jersey.

Bourne shell was the first shell to appear on Unix systems, thus it is referred to as "the shell".

Bourne shell is usually installed as /bin/sh on most versions of Unix. For this reason, it is the shell of choice for writing scripts that can be used on different versions of Unix.

The basic concept of a shell script is a list of commands, which are listed in the order of execution. A good shell script will have comments, preceded by '#' sign, describing the steps.

There are conditional tests, such as value A is greater than value B, loops allowing us to go through massive amounts of data, files to read and store data, and variables to read and store data, and the script may include functions.

We are going to write many scripts in the next sections. It would be a simple text file in which we would put all our commands and several other required constructs that tell the shell environment what to do and when to do it. Shell scripts and functions are both interpreted. This means they are not compiled.

Shell scripts have several required constructs that tell the shell environment what to do and when to do it. Of course, most scripts are more complex than the above one.

The shell is a real programming language, complete with variables, control structures, and so forth. No matter how complicated a script gets, it is still just a list of commands executed sequentially.

The following script uses the read command which takes the input from the keyboard and assigns it as the value of the variable PERSON and finally prints it on STDOUT.

That is why the Unix/GNU Linux shell is more powerful compared to the Windows shell.

There are some popular Linux shells, for example: Bash Shell, Tcsh/Csh Shell, Ksh Shell, Zsh Shell, Fish and so on.

1. Bash Shell

Bash Shell stands for Bourne Again Shell and it is the default shell on many Linux distributions today. It is also a sh-compatible shell and offers practical improvements over 'sh' for programming and interactive use, including:

- Command line editing

- Job Control

- Unlimited size command history

- Shell Functions and Aliases

- Unlimited size Indexed arrays

- Integer arithmetic in any base from two to sixty-four

Here is the picture example of the Linux Bash Shell:

```
BASH(1)                    General Commands Manual                    BASH(1)

NAME
       bash - GNU Bourne-Again SHell

SYNOPSIS
       bash [options] [command_string | file]

COPYRIGHT
       Bash is Copyright (C) 1989-2013 by the Free Software Foundation, Inc.

DESCRIPTION
       Bash is an sh-compatible command language interpreter that executes
       commands read from the standard input or from a file. Bash also incor-
       porates useful features from the Korn and C shells (ksh and csh).

       Bash is intended to be a conformant implementation of the Shell and
       Utilities portion of the IEEE POSIX specification (IEEE Standard
       1003.1). Bash can be configured to be POSIX-conformant by default.

OPTIONS
       All of the single-character shell options documented in the descrip-
       tion of the set builtin command can be used as options when the shell
 Manual page bash(1) line 1 (press h for help or q to quit)
```

2. Tcsh/Csh Shell

Tcsh is enhanced C shell, it can be used as an interactive login shell and shell script command processor.

Tcsh shell has the following characteristics

- C like syntax

- Command-line editor

- Programmable word and filename completion

- Spelling correction

- Job control

164

Here is the picture example of Linux Tsch/Csh shell:

```
TCSH(1)                        General Commands Manual                        TCSH(1)

NAME
       tcsh - C shell with file name completion and command line editing

SYNOPSIS
       tcsh [-bcdefFimnqstvVxX] [-Dname[=value]] [arg ...]
       tcsh -l

DESCRIPTION
       tcsh  is  an enhanced but completely compatible version of the Berkeley
       UNIX C shell, csh(1).  It is a command language interpreter usable both
       as an interactive login shell and a shell script command processor.  It
       includes a command-line editor (see The command-line editor),  program-
       mable word completion (see Completion and listing), spelling correction
       (see Spelling correction), a history mechanism (see  History  substitu-
       tion),  job  control  (see Jobs) and a C-like syntax.  The NEW FEATURES
       section describes major enhancements of tcsh over  csh(1).   Throughout
       this  manual, features of tcsh not found in most csh(1) implementations
       (specifically, the 4.4BSD csh) are labeled  with  `(+)',  and  features
       which are present in csh(1) but not usually documented are labeled with
       `(u)'.

Manual page tcsh(1) line 1 (press h for help or q to quit)█
```

3. Ksh Shell

Ksh stands for Korn shell and was designed and developed by David G. Korn. It is a complete, powerful, high-level programming language and also an interactive command language just like many other Unix/GNU Linux shells.

```
KSH(1)                  General Commands Manual                KSH(1)

NAME
        ksh, ksh93 - KornShell, a command and programming language

SYNOPSIS
        ksh  [  ±abcefhikmnoprstuvxBCDP ] [ -R file ] [ ±o option ] ... [ - ] [
        arg ... ]
        rksh [ ±abcefhikmnoprstuvxBCD ] [ -R file ] [ ±o option ] ... [ - ] [
        arg ... ]

DESCRIPTION
        Ksh  is  a command and programming language that executes commands read
        from a terminal or a file.  Rksh is a restricted version of the command
        interpreter  ksh;  it is used to set up login names and execution envi-
        ronments whose capabilities are more controlled than those of the stan-
        dard  shell.   Rpfksh  is a profile shell version of the command inter-
        preter ksh; it is used to to execute commands with the attributes spec-
        ified by the user's profiles (see pfexec(1)).  See Invocation below for
        the meaning of arguments to the shell.

   Definitions.
        A metacharacter is one of the following characters:
Manual page ksh(1) line 1 (press h for help or q to quit)
```

4. Zsh Shell

Zsh Shell is designed to be interactive and it incorporates many features of other Unix/GNU Linux shells such as bash, tcsh and ksh.

It is also a powerful scripting language just like the other shells available. Though it has some unique features, including:

- Filename generation

- Startup files

- Login/Logout watching

- Closing comments

- Concept index

- Variable index

- Functions index

Key index and many more that you can find out in man pages

```
ZSH(1)                       General Commands Manual                       ZSH(1)

NAME
       zsh - the Z shell

OVERVIEW
       Because  zsh contains many features, the zsh manual has been split into
       a number of sections:

       zsh         Zsh overview (this section)
       zshroadmap  Informal introduction to the manual
       zshmisc     Anything not fitting into the other sections
       zshexpn     Zsh command and parameter expansion
       zshparam    Zsh parameters
       zshoptions  Zsh options
       zshbuiltins Zsh built-in functions
       zshzle      Zsh command line editing
       zshcompwid  Zsh completion widgets
       zshcompsys  Zsh completion system
       zshcompctl  Zsh completion control
       zshmodules  Zsh loadable modules
       zshcalsys   Zsh built-in calendar functions
       zshtcpsys   Zsh built-in TCP functions
Manual page zsh(1) line 1 (press h for help or q to quit)
```

5. Fish

Fish in full stands for "friendly interactive shell" and was
authored in 2005. It was designed to be fully interactive and

user friendly. Just like the other shells, it has some pretty good features, including:

- Man page completions

- Web based configuration

- Auto-suggestions

- Fully scriptable with clean scripts

- Support for term256 terminal technology

Here is an example of the Linux fish shell:

```
fish(1)                            fish                            fish(1)

NAME
       fish - fish - the friendly interactive shell

fish - the friendly interactive shell
   Synopsis
       fish [-h] [-v] [-c command] [FILE [ARGUMENTS...]]

   Description
       fish is a command-line shell written mainly with interactive use in
       mind. The full manual is available in HTML by using the help command
       from inside fish.

       The following options are available:

       · -c or --command=COMMANDS evaluate the specified commands instead of
         reading from the commandline

       · -d or --debug-level=DEBUG_LEVEL specify the verbosity level of fish.
         A higher number means higher verbosity. The default level is 1.

       · -h or --help display help and exit
Manual page fish(1) line 1 (press h for help or q to quit)
```

These are not all the shells available in Unix/GNU Linux but they are the top most used and the most popular from those that are already installed on different Linux distributions.

Chapter 12: Introduction to Scripting

S hell scripts are just set of commands that you can write in a file and run them together. You can just put a series of commands into a text file and run them together. The difference comes from the fact that bash scripts can do a lot more than batch files.

Usually shells are interactive that mean, they accept command as input from users and execute them. However, some time we want to execute a bunch of commands routinely, so we have type in all commands each time in terminal.

As shell can also take commands as input from file, you can write these commands in a file and can execute them in shell to avoid this repetitive work. These files are called Shell Scripts or Shell Programs. Shell scripts are similar to the batch file in MS-DOS. Each shell script is saved with .sh file extension eg. myscript.sh

A shell script has syntax just like any other programming language. If you have any prior experience with any programming language like Python, C/C++ etc. it would be very easy to get started with it.

Shell scripting is writing a series of command for the shell to execute. It can combine lengthy and repetitive sequences of commands into a single and simple script, which can be stored and executed anytime. This reduces the effort required by the end user.

A shell script included some elements:

- Shell Keywords – if, else, break etc.

- Shell commands – cd, ls, echo, pwd, touch etc.

- Functions

- Control flow – 'if' 'then' 'else' cases and shell loops etc.

There are so many reasons why you should write shell scripts. If you want to avoid repetitive work and automation, then you should create a Linux shell script.

The shell scripting is also important for system admins who can use shell scripting for routine backups and similar things. Linux shell scripting is also used for system monitoring and protection as adding new functionality to the shell and similar.

The command and syntax are exactly the same as those directly entered in command line, so programmer do not need to switch to entirely different syntax. The writing shell scripts are much quicker and provide quick start with ability for interactive debugging.

But also, here are some disadvantages related to Linux scripting.

The scripting is prone to costly mistakes where a single mistake can change the command which might be terrible and make you a headache. There is also a slow execution speed that seems to be really frustrating while you are working on the projects. Designing flaws within the language syntax or implementation and not well suited for large and complex task are potential issues that you might face it.

Writing scripts

The first line called a "hashbang" or "shebang". It tells Unix that this script should be run through the /bin/bash shell. Second line is just the echo statement, which prints the words after it to the terminal. After saving the above file, we need to give it execute permission to make it runnable.

To process data, data must be kept in the computer's memory. Memory is separated into small locations and each location had a unique number called memory address, which is used to hold data.

Programmers can give a unique name to this memory address called variables. Variables are a named storage location that may take different values, but only one at a time.

In Linux Shell Scripting, there are two types of variable: System variables and User defined variable

System variables are created and are maintained by Linux itself. This type of variable defined in capital letters.

System variables can be used in the script to show any information these variables are holding. There are some important System variables:

- BASH — Holds the shell name

- BASH_VERSION — Holds the shell version name

- HOME — Holds home directory path

- OSTYPE — Holds Operating System type

- USERNAME – Holds username who is currently logged in to the machine

User-defined variables are as simple as we have in any other programming language, but variables can store any type of data, for example: name=abc

Almost all languages have the concept of loops. If we want to repeat a task ten times, we don't want to type the same code ten times, with maybe a slight change each time.

As a result, we have for and while loops in the shell scripting. This is somewhat fewer features than other languages.

The 'FOR' loop creates for example variable 'i' and assign a number to it from the list of number from 1 to n (any number). The shell executes echo statement for each assignment of 'i' variable and on every iteration, it will echo the statement as shown in the output. This process will continue until the last item in the loop counting.

The 'WHILE' loop will be executing until the condition is true. If this statement is removed the loop will be an infinite loop.

Function is a type of procedure or routine. Functions encapsulate a task with combining many instructions into a single line of code. Most programming languages provide many built-in functions that would otherwise require many steps to accomplish, for example calculating the square of a number.

In shell scripting, we can define functions in two manners:

- Creating a function inside the same script file to use.

- Create a separate file i.e. library.sh with all useful functions.

The exit command terminates a script, just as in a C program. It can also return a value, which is available to the script's parent process.

Every command returns an exit status referred as a return status or exit code. A successful command returns a zero, while an unsuccessful one returns a non-zero value that usually can be interpreted as an error code. Well-behaved UNIX commands, programs, and utilities return a zero-exit code upon successful completion though there are some exceptions.

When a script ends with an exit that has no parameter, the exit status of the script is the exit status of the last command executed in the script. The variable '$?' is a special variable in the Linux shell that reads the exit status of the last command executed. After a function returns, the variable '$?' give the exit status of the last command executed in the function.

There are some tips and tricks for starting a Linux shell scripting, for example:

- To get a Linux shell, you need to start a terminal.

- To see what shell you have, run: echo $SHELL.

- In Linux, the dollar sign ($) stands for a shell variable.

- The 'echo' command just returns whatever you type in.

- The pipeline instruction (|) comes to rescue, when chaining several commands.

- Linux commands have their own syntax, Linux won't forgive you whatsoever is the mistakes. If you get a command wrong, you won't flunk or damage anything, but it won't work.

- #!/bin/sh – It is called shebang. It is written at the top of a shell script and it passes the instruction to the program /bin/sh.

Chapter 13: Linux administration and security

Linux server administration and management is vital for any organization or individual who runs some kind of servers with 24/7 access to that server. Monitoring your critical service is vital for any business or organization if it wants to operate normally.

System administrators and IT professionals have deep knowledge of Linux network configuration and services as well as related fields such as basic security and performance. The need for System admins with advanced administration and networking skills has never been great and competition for people with experience is fierce.

The main characteristic that every System admin need to own are:

- Designing, deploying and maintaining a network running under Linux

- Administering the network services

- Skills to create and operate a network in any major Linux distributions

- Securely configuring the network interfaces

- Deploying and configuring file, web, email and name servers.

In recent years, Microsoft has responded to growing customer demand and developed software and services to run on Linux. Microsoft added support for major Linux distributions on its Azure public cloud platform, introduced Bash shell to the Windows 10 Enterprise operating system and joined the Linux Foundation as a Platinum member.

Most IT workers may never use the Windows Bash shell, but there are still plenty of other reasons why Windows admins should learn Linux administration. In 2016, Microsoft made PowerShell, its automation and configuration tool, an open source project that can run on Linux and Mac OS platforms.

In 2016, Microsoft shared that it will release a Linux version of its SQL Server database application. It is only a matter of time before Windows admins will need to support Microsoft server applications tailored to run on Linux servers.

Securing your Linux server is important to protect your data, intellectual property, and time from the hands of hackers and uninvited guests. The system administrator is responsible for security of the Linux box.

All data transmitted over a network is open to monitoring. Encrypt transmitted data whenever possible with password or using keys or certificates for better protection. Use scp, ssh, rsync, or sftp for file transfer. You can also mount remote server file system or your own home directory using special sshfs and fuse tools.

- GnuPG allows you to encrypt and sign your data and communication, features a versatile key management system as well as access modules for all kind of public key directories.

- OpenVPN is a cost-effective, lightweight SSL VPN. Another option is to try out tinc that uses tunneling and encryption to create a secure private network between hosts on the Internet or private insecure LAN.

- Lighttpd SSL (Secure Server Layer) Https Configuration And Installation

- Apache SSL (Secure Server Layer) Https Configuration And Installation

Avoid installing unnecessary software to avoid vulnerabilities in the software. Use the RPM package manager such as yum or apt-get or dpkg to review all installed set of software packages on a system. Delete all unwanted packages for better performance.

Running different network services on separate servers or VM instance will also make your Linux system security more effective. This limits the number of other services that can be compromised. For example, if an attacker is able to successfully exploit a software such as Apache flow, he or she will get an access to entire server including other services such as MySQL, MariaDB, PGSql, e-mail server and so on.

Always Keep Linux Kernel and software up to date. Applying security patches is an important part of maintaining Linux server. Linux provides all necessary tools to keep your system updated and also allows for easy upgrades between versions. All security update should be reviewed and applied as soon as possible. Again, use the RPM package manager such as yum and/or apt-get and/or dpkg to apply all security updates.

You can configure Red hat, CentOS, Fedora Linux, to send yum package update notification via email. Another option is to apply all security updates via a 'cron' job. Under Debian or Ubuntu Linux you can use 'apticron' to send security notifications. It is also possible to configure unattended upgrades for your Debian or Ubuntu Linux server using 'apt-get' command or just 'apt' command. Here is an example:

$ sudo apt-get install unattended-upgrades apt-listchanges bsd-mailx

Linux comes with various security patches which can be used to guard against misconfigured or compromised programs. If it possible, you can use SELinux and other Linux security extensions to enforce limitations on network and other programs. For example, SELinux provides a variety of security policies for Linux kernel.

Using SELinux will provide a flexible Mandatory Access Control (MAC). Under standard Linux Discretionary Access Control (DAC), an application or process running as a user (UID or SUID) has the user's permissions to objects such as files, sockets, and other processes. Running a MAC kernel protects the system from malicious or flawed applications that can damage or destroy the system.

For better security insurance, use the 'useradd' or 'usermod' commands to create and maintain user accounts. Make sure you have a good and strong password policy. For example, a good password includes at least 8 characters long and mixture of alphabets, number, special character, upper and lower alphabets etc. The most important, pick a password you can remember. Use tools such as "John the ripper" to find out weak users passwords on your server.

The 'chage' command changes the number of days between password changes and the date of the last password change. This information is used by the system to determine when a user must change his/her password. The 'etc' or 'login.defs' file defines the site-specific configuration for the shadow password suite including password aging configuration. Here is the command example: # chage -M 99999 userName

You can also prevent all users from using or reuse same old passwords under Linux. The 'pan unix' module and parameter remember can be used to configure the number of previous passwords that cannot be reused.

Under Linux you can use the faillog command to display faillog records or to set login failure limits. 'faillog' formats the contents of the failure log from var, log, faillog database with log file. It also can be used for maintains failure counters and limits. Here is the example: faillog -r -u username

Never login as root user. You should use 'sudo' to execute root level commands as and when required. sudo does greatly enhances the security of the system without sharing root password with other users and admins. sudo provides simple auditing and tracking features too.

You must protect Linux servers physical console access. Configure the BIOS and disable the booting from external devices such as DVDs, CDs, USB pen and similar. Set BIOS and grub boot loader password to protect these settings. All production boxes must be locked in Internet Data Centers and all persons must pass some sort of security checks before accessing your server.

That were the most popular and the most used Linux security tips for better system protection and data secure. You can use these advices to make your Linux operating system more protected and raise your system security.

Chapter 14: Linux Internet Connecting

On Linux, the desktop environment automatically connects to the internet. It can be connected to Wi-Fi or Ethernet network. This is great, but if you need to access the internet via the command line, it doesn't let you.

Connecting to the internet from the command line over Ethernet can be really complex. Users will need to manually turn on an individual network device, assign it an IP address, set up the DNS settings, subnet and etc. Nobody has time for that. Luckily, there's a quick and easy way to get this going.

Keep in mind, if your Linux PC does not have an internet connection, you won't be able to quickly install dhcpcd5 packages. Instead, you will need to check for loadable binaries, download the files and then load them up while offline. Check to see if your PC has dhcpcd by running it in the terminal. If the terminal repeats "command not found", or something similar it is not on the system. Debian or Ubuntu may require 'dhcpcd5' while others use 'dhcpcd'.

The graphical Network Manager Connection tool has a console mode. With it, connecting to wireless networks via the command line is easier than ever.

First, be sure that you've already got network manager installed. This shouldn't be a problem as just about every Linux operating system makes use of Network Manager. If for some reason it is not installed, refer to your operating system's manual on how to enable it. Next, run a scan inside 'nmcli' for nearby wireless networks.

Using nmcli with "device Wi-Fi list" will print out a detailed list of all wireless networks that the user can access, complete with SSIDs, channels, connection modes, signal strength and etc. Connect to any one of these networks using "nmcli device Wi-Fi connect".

Once connected, be sure to run the ping command to verify you have an internet connection with the command: ping google.com -c3

There are list some simple steps how to connect Wi-Fi network with your Linux distro.

- Open the System Menu on the right side of the top bar.

- Click on Wi-Fi Not Connected to expand the menu.

- Click on Select Network.

- Look through the names of the nearby networks. Select the one you want. If you don't see the name of the network you want, click More to see additional networks. If you still don't see the network you want, it may be hidden or you may be out of range.

- Enter the password for the network and click Connect.

Chapter 15: Benefits Of The Linux Operating System

Linux is an operating system just like Windows; Mac OS X developed by Linus Torvalds in 1991. Linux was just an operating system but now it became the platform to run desktops, embedded systems, and servers. It was developed as an alternative for Minix Linux has many variations and distributions because of its modular design and provides many advantages over other operating systems and that is why it is used almost in every field nowadays, from smartphones to supercomputers, cars to home appliances and many more.

One of the main advantages of Linux is that it is an open source operating system. Its source code is easily available for everyone. Anyone capable of coding can contribute, modify, enhance and distribute the code to anyone and for any purpose.

Linux is more secure in comparison to other operating systems such as Windows. Linux is not completely secure as there is some malware for it also, but it is less vulnerable than others. Every program in Linux whether an application or a virus, need authorization from the administrator in the form of a password. Unless the password is typed virus won't execute. There is no requirement of any anti-virus program in Linux.

In Linux you encounter a larger number of software updates. These software updates are much faster than updates in any other operating system. Updates in Linux can be done easily without facing any major issue or concern.

There are also many distributions available called distros of Linux. It provides various choices or flavors to the users. You can select any bistros according to your needs. Some distros of Linux are Fedora, Ubuntu, Arch Linux, Debian, Linux Mint and many more. If you are a beginner, you can use Ubuntu or Linux Mint. If you are a good programmer, you may use Debian or Fedora.

Linux is freely available on the web to download and use. You do not need to buy the license for it as Linux and many of its software come with GNU General Public License.

This proved to be one of the major advantages Linux faces over Windows and other operating systems. You need to spend a huge amount to buy the license of Windows which is not the case with Linux.

Linux provides high stability also this is good advantage. It does not need to be rebooted after a short period of time. Your Linux system rarely slows down or freezes. As in windows, you need to reboot your system after installing or uninstalling an application or updating your software but this is not the case with Linux. You can work without any disturbance on your Linux systems.

Linux ensures the privacy of user's data as it never collects much data from the user while using its distributions or software, but this is not true for many other operating systems.

Linux provides a high range of flexibility as you can install only required components. There is no need to install a full or complete suite. You can also keep Linux file under multiple partitions so if one of them corrupts then there is no major loss. You only need to repair that particular partition, not the complete file which is not the case with other operating systems.

This operating system can be easily installed from the web and does not require any prerequisites as it can run on any hardware, even on your oldest systems.

This is also a multitasking operating system and it can perform many tasks simultaneously without any decrease in its speed such as downloading a large file would not slow down the system.

Linux provides various desktop environments to make it easy to use. While installing Linux you can choose any desktop environment according to your wishes such as KDE (K Desktop Environment) or GNOME (GNU Network Object Model Environment).

It also runs or executes all possible file formats and is compatible with a large number of file formats.

Conclusion

After reading this Linux guide, I hope that you gain more knowledge about the most important things you should know about Linux operating system and its benefits.

Linux is the most popular and the most used open source operating system, built and distributed by Linus Torvalds in 1991. This operating system comes with Linux distribution named as Linux Kernel - supporting system software with additional libraries.

The world's usage of this operating system is really high thanks to the various Linux distributions acceptable for every user depending on their job, working projects, needs and desires. There is also a huge step by step process of how to download and install Linux operating system on your device, in package to the chosen distribution.

There was also and detail description of the Linux distros and which one is perfectly matched with your personal computer needs, expectations and similar things, whether it is Ubuntu, Fedora, Debian, openSUSE etc...

I hope you have learnt more about the famous Linux command line and now you can use it with no problem. There were included the most used commands and codes that will help you to work on the new Linux environment and how to maintenance your distribution performances related to your needs and desires.

Also, you had the chance to learn more about Linux applications and packaged software that are included with its installation together with the chosen distribution, for example: Partition Manager, Education Software, GIMP photo editor, Libre Office tool, Google Drives, Linux security software and so on.

I hope that you enjoyed Linux for Beginners and made your knowledge deeper than before.

Mark Solomon Brown

www.ingramcontent.com/pod-product-compliance
Lightning Source LLC
Chambersburg PA
CBHW071118050326
40690CB00008B/1264